A Very Short, Fairly Interesting and Reasonably Cheap Book About Studying Strategy

Chris Carter, Stewart R. Clegg and
Martin Kornberger

WITHDRAWN

Los Angeles | London | New Delhi

© Chris Carter, Stewart Clegg and Martin Kornberger 2008

First published 2008
Reprinted 2009

SAGE Publications Ltd
1 Oliver's Yard
55 City Road
London EC1Y 1SP

SAGE Publications Inc.
2455 Teller Road
Thousand Oaks, California 91320

SAGE Publications India Pvt Ltd
B 1/I 1 Mohan Cooperative Industrial Area
Mathura Road
New Delhi 110 044

SAGE Publications Asia-Pacific Pte Ltd
33 Pekin Street #02-01
Far East Square
Singapore 048763

Library of Congress Control Number: 2008922367

British Library Cataloguing in Publication data

A catalogue record for this book is available from
the British Library

ISBN 978-1-4129-4786-2
ISBN 978-1-4129-4787-9 (pbk)

Typeset by C&M Digitals (P) Ltd, Chennai, India
Printed in Great Britain by The Athenaeum Press, Gateshead
Printed on paper from sustainable resources

Dedication

For my wife Ingrid – Chris
For Lynne, Jonathon & William – Stewart
For Jess – Martin

Contents

Acknowledgements

We have enjoyed the support and collegiality of a number of friends in the production of this short book. The book was written in 2007, and for much of that period Aston Business School provided a congenial and creative backdrop for Stewart. Aston also generously funded a workshop on strategy and we would like, especially, to mention Mike West. At the University of St Andrews, Nic Beech, J. Ignacio Canales, Alan McKinlay, Frank Mueller, Crawford Spence and John 'the acceptable face of economics' Wilson were all supporters of the project. Barbara Lessels was very helpful in getting the bibliography fixed up. Edinburgh was an important meeting point at crucial stages of the project. Walks around the city, visits to hostelries frequented by DI John Rebus – an activity known as Rebusing – and marvellous dinners hosted by Ingrid and Mama Jeacle were an important backdrop to the production of this book. Equally, Balmain and Haberfield in Sydney were important contexts for shaping many of the ideas in the book. Elsewhere, Richard Badham (Macquarie University), Peter Clark (University of London), Will Clegg, Claire Davidson, Jerry Gent and Keith Hoskin (Warwick Business School) were all enthusiastic supporters of the project. Jerry Gent merits a special mention for showing Chris around Machiavelli's Florence in the summer of 2007. The book was finalized on Bill and Joyce Clegg's veranda in Bongaree on beautiful Bribie Island in Queensland, and we want to acknowledge their help and hospitality in supporting the final writing. Finally, Kiren Shoman of Sage was a great advocate of the project and we thank her for its commissioning.

Once Upon a Time ...

introduction

Not only is the book very short, fairly interesting and reasonably cheap, but it is also quite comprehensive. In these pages we will provide an overview of what has become one of the most influential fields of management: strategy.

We begin in this chapter with an overview of strategy, discussing some of its auspices and influences, and identify some of the key issues: where strategy comes from; how it operates; it's relation to competition; and why there are so many definitions of what the key terms mean.

the ubiquitousness of strategy

Strategy is everywhere. Soccer teams have strategies, as do political parties, and, more personally, people have strategies for making themselves available when they desire to create an interest in someone – and they usually have strategies for handling the inevitable rebuttals that ensue. And of course, organizations have strategies – or they are supposed to. In management and organization theory, the contemporary focus on strategy reflects significant changes in the corporate environment that have occurred in recent decades. Strategy is cast as the main job of executives in organizations, transcending the mere operational detail of finance, human resources, marketing, etc. Our colleague Stefano Harney (2007), who teaches strategy at the University of London, has characterized strategy as the queen of the management sciences, the sovereign subject. Like us, he thinks that it is time to explore the legitimacy of its claims to sovereignty.

As students of management, it is important to be able to read and understand the language of strategy. Especially if you are an ambitious student of management! The reason is simple: strategy occupies the commanding heights of the organization and if you aim to reach for the top this is where you will want to be.

So what is strategy? While many read the discourse of strategy as something stretching back into ancient history, strategy has an interesting duality. The idea of strategy *can* be traced back to time immemorial and often is: in the work of Sun Tzu, for instance, whose early writings on military strategy in *The Art of War* are often said to be the birth of the discipline, and are available today in various versions and translations which sustain many pages of product at Amazon.com. Sun Tzu is merely the most ancient of a long line of putative predecessors that number in their ranks the Florentine political philosopher, Niccolò Machiavelli and the Prussian general, Carl von Clausewitz. If strategy is not traced to some long-dead Chinese mandarin, Florentine diplomat or Prussian general, it is often traced to some long-dead Greek philosopher. One of the ways that academic areas seek to accrue legitimacy is through creating such genealogies. The judicious choice of ancestors is an old marketing trick. The idea that strategy may be traced in a seamless continuity of development from the ancient Greeks 500 years before the birth of Christ to the current day *is* patently absurd. Machiavelli and Clausewitz *did* strategize, but in a very different context and with different objectives in mind. There is no straightforward linear history of accumulated and progressive building of a coherent body of knowledge. In fact, whatever coherence there is, it is very much an attempt at retrospective sensemaking, an attempt to construct a legitimate intellectual pedigree for a body of knowledge that is an intellectual mongrel. Taking history a bit more seriously, we'll see how strategy changes and develops. As a conscious management discourse, strategy is a relatively recent phenomenon (with, of course, a grand teleology now invented for it!). Essentially, it is a post-Second World War, largely US invention, with undoubted roots in military thinking.

The influence of military planning on strategy cannot be emphasized enough, which is not surprising. The military has been a great source of strategic lessons, from the outset of the field. Keith Hoskin and Richard MacVe (1986, 1988), for instance, have highlighted the way in which strategy as a discipline emerged from military ideas.

In the late nineteenth and twentieth centuries American corporations grew inexorably larger and as a consequence needed to develop new means of managing. Ideas and models were borrowed from military planners.

Armies were the first rapidly moving organizations that faced an enemy which threatened them. As organizations grew bigger and competition becomes fiercer, military strategy was seen as an appropriate backdrop for talk and action in corporate boardrooms. The macho talk also suited the identities of many strategists in large corporations, who were happy to imagine themselves as warriors or field marshals directing a war. War with competitors, battles for mind- and market-share and the quest for domination evolved and shaped these conversations that are labelled 'strategic'.

War teaches Strategy. The Battle of Cannae in 216BC was a classic case of how a double envelopment/encirclement by Hannibal allowed him to beat a Roman Army of almost twice the size. In December 1805 Napoleon's greatest victory, at Austerlitz, was made with the 'Lion Leap', a flanking attack through the morning fog by the fourth corps, led by Nicolas Soult. These strategies and tactics are still taught at Sandhurst and West Point as a way of managing large static armies. They worked well until the 1914–18 war, when it was found that a couple of strategically placed machine guns could hold up foot soldiers on the move. Fully mechanized war did change the way generals thought, but it took time for their strategy to change in accordance with the new realities of technological warfare. Nowhere was this more evident than in the Battle of the Somme, a battle best remembered for its first day, 1 July 1916, on which the British suffered 57,470 casualties, including 19,240 dead – the bloodiest day in the history of the British Army. The British artillery was too light, too distant from the target, and the German fortifications were too sophisticated for much damage to be sustained by the prior bombardments that were supposed to have destroyed the German resolve. As the troops advanced, at a walking pace, they were simply mown down by the German machine guns. Those 57,470 casualties were a lesson in the inappropriateness of the strategy pursued, but it was not until the closing stages of the war, and the lessons of antipodean officers such as General Monash, that skilful planning and attention to detail led to the development of more effective strategies.

Interestingly, elsewhere in the British Empire, rebel fighters such as Michael Collins in Ireland were showing themselves adept at military strategy. Lloyd George, the then British Prime Minister, lamented that his home grown generals – later dubbed as donkeys – had none of the military wit or imagination of Collins. The Allied generals thought only of attrition until the Spring Offensive in 1918 when the Germans adopted Storm Trooper tactics, which enabled them to burst through the lines but, in the end, they found that they had advanced too far because they had outrun their own supply lines. The Germans learned from this in the Second World War but, by this time, they enjoyed the great advances of air power and the tank technology, with which to implement *Blitzkrieg* successfully.

Strategy, not only in war but in business, is driven by technology which can wipe out or reduce competition. While the days of finance-led businesses are not over, there is a huge challenge being driven by technology as a vast amount of business is done over the Web. A firm must now have an IT strategy, something that does not always sit well with older members of a Board, who know it is essential but fear it because it can inhibit their power and decision-making if they don't understand its ramifications.

It is perhaps not surprising that military metaphors are commonplace in the strategy literature, given its historical origins and the way in which these have been used to account for it in contemporary terms. While the preoccupation with war is understandable, we argue that it is in need of revision. There is nothing heroic or glorious about war, as any old soldier will tell you – a cursory look at current events in Iraq being a sobering instance of its folly. Of course, it was a commitment to the metaphors of war, of 'shock and awe', that talked the US government into Iraq in the first place.

competition entails strategy

While in the dim and distant past organizations might have pursued strategies, these were not articulated through the contemporary discourse of strategy, which, above all, emerged from organizations having to deal with issues of competition. If there was no competition, there would be no need for strategy. Where there is only a monopoly provider, then the monopolist is able to sell or distribute whatever quality of goods it wishes, without regard for strategy, because, if people want what it provides, they have to accept what is on offer. Competition immediately changes the picture. Porter, one of the most influential voices in strategy, actually based his book on competitive strategy on how to get closer to a monopolistic competition by taking the viewpoint of the firm (Porter, 1980).

Competition is the key: wherever similar products are sold in the same market there will be competition. Firms that thrive competitively develop strategy as an account of how they are doing what they do and what they are proposing to do. Where competitors sell largely undifferentiated products at similar prices, then it is imperative to be able to position specific products as having a specific difference. Think of The Hard Rock Café restaurants in the USA and elsewhere. The value proposition is the same old fast-food laden with fats and cholesterol but – wait for it – there are guitars and other instruments once used by long-gone musicians on the wall: fast food + nostalgia and a strange sense of community.

The competitive picture is brought into sharper focus where the market is not just for simple burgers and processed food and drinks, but is highly uncertain and rapidly changing. In a corporate environment that has become increasingly dynamic and complex, strategy is management's response to turbulence.

There is, however, a paradox of competition: the larger the organization, the less competition it is likely to encounter. Therefore, it might be that the organization's strategy, while shrouded in rhetoric about competition, is in fact seeking to avoid competitors. A good example of this would be the Scottish Banking sector which, until comparatively recently, saw a great deal of collusion between the different 'competitors'. The banks paid the same interest rates on deposit accounts, all agreed not to pay interest rates on current accounts, and did not attempt to poach either staff or customers from 'competitors'. While the financial services industry has undoubtedly changed, it is important to be aware that competition is not always what it seems. For instance, JJB sports, a large sports retailer, were fined £6.7 million by the Office of Fair Trading for price-fixing the cost of England and Manchester United football shirts between 2000 and 2001. Six other firms with whom they colluded were also fined. As the Office of Fair Trading put it, 'The Office of Fair Trading considers that agreements between undertakings that fix prices are among the most serious infringements of the Competition Act 1998' (http://www.oft.gov.uk/advice_and_resources/resource_base/ ca98/decisions/football-kit). At the time of writing, British Airways has just been fined a record £270 million for price-fixing its fuel surcharges on its transatlantic flights with Virgin Atlantic. In Australia, the countries third wealthiest billionaire, Richard Pratt, who owns Visy, the world's largest privately owned paper and cardboard manufacturer, has recently been charged in a cardboard box price-fixing scandal with competitors Amcor. So, strategy, at its most effective, from a short-term perspective, may well entail illegal activity. Few strategists, we suspect, are likely to recommend criminal activity to their readers, however effective it might be as a strategic gambit, but obviously, given these cases, some strategists do recommend such action!

Strategy is supposed to lead an organization through changes and shifts to secure its future growth and sustainable success. Without a clear strategy, organizations will drift, much as might a small yacht, disabled, without sails or rudder, on a storm-tossed sea. No steering capacity will be evident. Organizations in this respect are somewhat like governments: they steer not the ship of state but the fortunes of all those life chances, income and profits and losses, which are tied up in their good management. Just as, from time to time, governments appear rudderless, so do some organizations. For instance, one of the criticisms of John Major's government between 1990 and 1997 in the UK was that it lacked any strategic direction but just lurched from one crisis to the next. Before its recent renaissance the same things were being said about the doyenne of British retailers, Marks & Spencers (M&S), but then Stuart Rose reset its strategic direction by developing boutique brands within the general umbrella of M&S and hiring celebrity models for its marketing, such as Twiggy, Bryan Ferry and Take That.

As we mentioned earlier in this chapter, as a language game, strategy is everywhere. Corporations, politicians and sports teams talk of strategy. So do public sector organizations. One of the interesting developments in government organizations over the last twenty years has been the rise of 'New Public Management'. Broadly speaking, this has seen the incorporation of private sector 'managerialist' policies into the state sector. This change in rationality helps explain why a 'hospital patient' has become a 'customer', or a train passenger has become a 'customer'. Some universities even encourage their staff to see students as customers. The ushering in of managerialism to the public sector has fuelled the growth of strategy-making in government organizations. Organizations such as hospitals, schools and councils spend inordinate amounts of effort making strategy. They articulate their strategies through private sector strategy terminology. But of course, they do not exist in markets or have competitors, although increasingly they are subject to being ranked in league tables, which have the effect of a market. An executive in a hospital might therefore spend a lot of time plotting ways to improve its ranking in a league table (Mueller et al., 2003). Mike Power (1997) has referred to the whole move towards league tables as being about the rise of the audit society. Now you see why it's hardly surprising that strategic management is increasingly understood as *the* task of top management. To be able to say 'I set strategy' has great cachet. It marks out the top managers from the also-rans.

The story of strategy is very much the story of our times. There is a complex interplay between hope and fear. It is exciting but also fraught with danger; as Stefano Harney (2007) suggests, the emergence of the discourse of strategy is a key symptom signifying that all is not well with management. What he means is that business – for all its ingenuity – to the extent that it is premised on metaphors of war, will always comprise more losers than winners, as there only ever can be one winner while there can be many losers. Strategy offers an opening or a way for managers to appear to be doing something to win. In the end it matters little if the strategy succeeds or fails. What matters is that they have a strategy with which the realities of 'success' and 'failure' can be accounted. In a similar vein, Keith Hoskin (2007) has noted that a lot of the language associated with strategy is ebullient, hopeful and death-defying whereas the stories from practitioners are far more fragmented and are tales of woe, pointlessness and despair. Strategy is a discourse that is *useful* for papering over the fearsome cracks in a firm's rationality, for it holds the manager and the firm to account.

▨▨▨▨ defining strategy

Scholars have complained that 'strategy has become a catchall term used to mean whatever one wants it to mean' (Hambrick and Fredrickson, 2001: 49). We agree that there is a certain vagueness associated with the notion of strategy, but also note that, to date, the imagination of strategy researchers has been rather limited. Most researchers in the field use definitions that are as little different from each other as the products of the business schools they sit in.

Etymologically, the word 'strategy' derives from ancient Greek and consists of two parts: *stratos* meaning army, and *agein* meaning to lead (Cummings, 2003). Cummings argues that the term 'strategy' became important once warfare developed a certain complexity and forced commanders to coordinate relatively large sea and land forces. As we have seen above, it is only a short step from the world of military competition to the world of competing businesses. The word started to gain traction in the world of business in the 1950s as many executives with military experience in the Second World War sought to apply the long-range planning, characterizing events such as the Normandy Landings, to their business. The first authors who developed the notion of strategy into a more consistent business concept were titans of industry, such as Chester Barnard from AT&T, Alfred Sloan from General Motors and Alfred Dupont Chandler, the business historian, also related to the DuPont Chemicals family.

There are almost as many definitions of strategy as there are strategists. Why this should be so is obvious: it's good strategy for strategists as they all seek to position the field around their intellectual capital. It is not just a question of intellectual ego, either; strategy is big business, with a considerable capacity for consultancy earnings in the stratosphere if you find the gold at the end of the strategy rainbow. Ask Michael Porter. Let's look at some of the most commonly used definitions:

> Strategy can be defined as the determination of the basic long-term goals and objectives of an enterprise, and the adoption of courses of action and the allocation of resources necessary for carrying out these goals. (Chandler, 1962: 15)

> [Strategy is] the pattern of objectives, purposes or goals and major policies and plans for achieving these goals, stated in such a way as to

define what business the company is in, or is to be in and the kind of company it is or is to be. (Learned et al., 1969: 15)

Compare these definitions to a typical textbook definition. For instance, Thompson and Strickland (2006: 3) provide the following definition:

A company's strategy consists of the competitive moves and business approaches that managers employ to grow the business, stake out a market position, attract and please customers, compete successfully, conduct operations, and achieve targeted objectives.

Now look at one of the definitions from the field of International Relations:

... strategy is a process, a constant adaptation to shifting conditions and circumstances in a world where chance, uncertainty, and ambiguity dominate. Moreover, it is a world in which the actions, intentions, and purposes of other participants remain shadowy and indistinct, taxing the wisdom and intuition of the canniest policy maker. Carl von Clausewitz suggests that in such an environment, 'principles, rules, or even systems' of strategy must always fall short, undermined by the world's endless complexities. (Murray and Grimsley, 1994: 1)

Four characteristics are shared by these definitions across different disciplines:

- Strategy seems to be about the future and goals that you want to achieve in the future. It's a plan, a roadmap to the future. After all, if you don't have a goal you cannot score!
- It is somehow concerned with how to get to these goals. It talks about resources and the allocation of these that will get the organization from point A in the here and now to point B, a desired point in the future.
- It seems to be necessary to have strategies because of competition: if there was no competition, there would be no need for strategy. Because other firms fight for a slice of the same pie, you have to be smarter, better, faster than your competitors.
- It seems to be top management's business. Since strategy deals with the big picture and the future, it is very important business. And the people

who strategize consider themselves to be very important too. Usually it is a top management privilege to spend time at expensive retreats arguing with even more expensive consultants about 'what if ...' scenarios. Even universities do these things!

Although most of these definitions are useful, we would argue that they do not capture the ways that strategy can be and has been 'made up' or put together. One reason for this is that management in general and strategy in particular are very ahistorical disciplines. The relentless quest for the new and the claim to be at the forefront of whatever the fashion of the day might be makes looking back an ostensibly useless enterprise. For instance, many strategy scholars spend only a couple of pages on the history of strategy before they launch into the contemporary canon of strategic management.

It is possible to date business strategy as a self-conscious discipline as entirely a recent, post-Second World War enterprise. It is also possible to see it as merely the most contemporary outcrop of a characteristically political activity – steering an enterprise towards future horizons. Conceived this way, it is possible to argue that strategy is really just diplomacy applied in the commercial rather than the political sphere. If one maintains this argument, then the grandfather of strategists has to be Niccolò Machiavelli, the Florentine diplomat and author who lived from 1469 to 1527. For Machiavelli, the everyday art of statecraft was war by means other than the force of arms. Indeed, a prudent Prince would not rush to achieve by war what could, with guile, diplomacy and example, be achieved more readily by politics.

alternative histories of strategy

As the Danish philosopher Søren Kierkegaard once said, history is like prophecy – just directed backwards, not forwards in time. To quote Kierkegaard (1992) again, we live out lives much as a spider spins a thread to let itself down from the ceiling to the floor: we have nothing in front of us but as we travel through space we produce a thread, a narrative behind us. Strategy is similar. It produces arguments that strive to make sense of where we have come from and where we are heading for. Narratives *are* important. Looking at history tells us where we come from, at which point certain decisions were made, how they influenced things and, most importantly, how they could be changed, and this is as true of organizations as it is of states and individuals.

What are different historical perspectives on strategy? Why did the phenomenon become so important in our times? Where did it come from? We will argue that strategy's origins lie in what we call, for want of a better term, 'statecraft'. People such as Machiavelli implicitly strategized about how to run one of the largest organizations of their times, which were city-states. Although modern versions of strategy might look very different, we will argue that they derive from the same roots as Machiavelli's strategy. The latter is sometimes seen as a dark, misanthropic but bluntly honest account of what it means to be doing strategy. Indeed, the term 'Machiavellian' has passed into general usage as a term, mostly, of opprobrium. Machiavelli was a pragmatist and interested in *Realpolitick*, which was in contrast to romanticized notions around statecraft held by ancient philosophers such as Cicero.

Machiavelli's book *The Prince* (written around 1513) describes the forms and practices of governing a state that will be most successful. In the late 1400s, after the fall of the Medici regime, Machiavelli became a senior diplomat in the Florentine government (at a time where much of what is now Italy was divided into city-states as well as the papal state, which were often dominated by the French or Spanish). Florence was a world of shifting alliances, political intrigue and turbulence. During his period as a diplomat, Machiavelli travelled widely and met many of the important leaders of the day, including the pope, the French monarch and the king of Spain. Rubbing shoulders with the power brokers of the day increased Machiavelli's fascination with politics. An example of this is when he recalls:

> I discussed this matter at Nantes with the Cardinal of Rouen. ... When the Cardinal of Rouen remarked to me that Italians did not understand warfare, I replied that the French did not understand statecraft for if they did they would not have permitted the church to acquire so much power. And experience has shown that the power of both the Church and the King of Spain, here in Italy, has been brought about by the King of France, and they have brought about his ruin. (Machiavelli, 1988: 14)

In 1512, Machiavelli's world collapsed when the government he served capitulated to the Spanish, who then reinstalled the Medici regime. Things got worse for Machiavelli; he was arrested and tortured under suspicion of taking part in a plot against the new government. He was then exiled to his farm outside Florence, where he was to spend the rest of his life. This was a form of social death for Machiavelli, as he only returned to Florence, the place that so fascinated him, towards the end of his life. It was shortly after his exile that he wrote *The Prince*, which chronicled his observations of what made an effective ruler.

Dedicating the book to the new ruler of Florence (first, to Guilano de'Medici, who was recalled to Rome and then replaced by his nephew, Lorenzo de'Medici, to whom the book was re-dedicated!), Machiavelli probably hoped that his text would bring him back into public affairs. Indeed, he promised in the foreword that the book was a means of helping the Medici achieve greatness. However, Machiavelli did not return to the hurly burly of public affairs, so his strategy failed, yet his legacy is a text still relevant to strategy and statecraft. The book switches between ancient history, in which the literati of the day would have been schooled, and contemporary politics, which of course is now medieval history! Though he discusses issues in general terms, there can be no doubt he is thinking and writing about Florence.

Machiavelli wrote the book in times of great political turmoil, when Italy was divided into many city-states that either were conquered or were conquering one another, with shifting support (and success) from the German, the Spanish and the French rulers as well as from the Vatican. Being involved in negotiations between senior state officials, Machiavelli was less interested in the ceremony of governing than in the reality of politics. As he puts it: 'the main foundation of every state … are good laws and good arms; and because you cannot have good laws without good arms, and where there are good arms, good laws inevitably follow, I shall not discuss laws but give my attention to arms' (1988: 77). Implicitly, Machiavelli criticizes theories on governance that are based on contracts, laws and notions of virtue. For him, it is the power to be able to implement a law that makes the law in the first place: policy follows power. For him, the two types of engagement (law and force) correspond with human nature – the man and the beast in us. The leader must know how 'to make nice use of the beast and the man' (1988: 99). As we will see, strategy has as much to do with the beast, or the dark side in us, as with the more noble, civilized and human side. Machiavelli develops a deep critique of many of the established 'statecraft' texts, such as those by the ancient philosophers Cicero and Seneca. Both of these writers were hugely influential and espoused that a leader should rule virtuously. Their influence was found in the advice manuals produced by some of Machiavelli's contemporaries, who again emphasized virtuous and civilized behaviour. Machiavelli pointed to a series of paradoxes around virtue. For instance, he points out the difficulties of a ruler being generous: 'There is nothing that is so self-consuming as generosity: the more you practise it, the less you will be able to continue to practise it. You will either become poor and despised or your efforts to avoid poverty will make you rapacious and hated; and being generous will lead to both' (Machiavelli, 1988: 57).

Machiavelli makes this point very clear: a prince 'must have no other object or thought, nor acquire skill in anything, except war, its organization, and its discipline' (1988: 87). Machiavelli elaborates on physical and mental exercises that shape a leader's mind: he must engage in practical geography, studying marshes, mountains, plains, hills, rivers, etc. Intellectually, a ruler must study 'the actions of eminent men to see how they conducted themselves during war' (1988: 89). Think of those biographies of successful business leaders such as Jack Welch and their heroic tales of turnaround and growth!

Machiavelli developed a practical manual of strategic and tactical advice that allows leaders to govern their states effectively. Machiavelli wrote that sensing troubles is the key to successful strategy: 'as the doctors say of a wasting disease, to start with, it is easy to cure but difficult to diagnose; after a time ... it becomes easy to diagnose but difficult to cure' (1988: 39). Hence, one has to take counter-measures as soon as troubles are visible on the horizon. Machiavelli uses the Romans as example: they never avoided war 'because they knew that there is no avoiding war; it can only be postponed to the advantage of others' (1988: 40). For Machiavelli, power, conflict and war are at the centre of strategy. Power struggles cannot be avoided.

Machiavelli portrays Cesare Borgia, son of the pope and feared prince of his times, as an example of extraordinary strategic foresight. Cesare was extremely successful in acquiring resources for and enlarging his state through wars. His major ally was his father, Pope Alexander VI. To demonstrate the strategic thinking of Cesare, Machiavelli explains how he guarded against the possibility of a hostile successor to the papacy that would not support him. First, he destroyed all the families of the rulers he had despoiled so the new pope could not develop alliances with them against him. Second, he made friends with all the patricians in Rome. Third, he controlled the College of Cardinals as far as he could (because it controlled the pope). Finally, he acquired enough power to withstand a direct attack. Machiavelli praises Cesare as a strategic mind who focused on exactly those things that allowed him to enlarge and strengthen his empire.

From an ethical perspective we might not agree with the idea of destroying families as a strategic move to secure power. Even though he was no sentimentalist, Machiavelli realized that what strategy dictated prudence might counsel against. Yet, *Realpolitik* does not allow for too much pondering. He believed that cruelty can be used well or badly: if it is employed fast, used once and for all, and one's safety depends on it, it is being used well (1988: 65). In a similar vein, he argues that it is far better to be feared than loved: 'The bond of love is one which men, wretched creatures that they are, break when it is to their advantage to do so; but fear is strengthened by a dread of punishment which is always effective' (1988: 97). A last example of the pragmatic stance that Machiavelli takes towards strategy was his perspective on how a leader should honour his word. He acknowledged that it is praiseworthy to honour one's word. He continues: 'nonetheless contemporary experience shows that princes who have achieved great things have been those who have given their word lightly, who have known how to trick men with their cunning, and who, in the end, have overcome those abiding by honest principles' (1988: 99). Therefore he concludes that a ruler 'cannot, and must not, honour his word when it places him at a disadvantage and when the reasons for which he made his promise no longer exists' (1988: 100). Think of modern politicians – how true is Machiavelli's description!

Machiavelli knows how important it is to display good qualities and hide others. For Machiavelli, the ruler must not let good qualities hinder successful rule. In fact, ethicality can be harmful. A Prince should *appear* to have good qualities, however: 'men in general judge by their eyes rather than by their hands; because everyone is in a position to watch, few are in a position to come in close touch with you. Everyone sees what you appear to be, few experience what you really are' (1988: 101). Hence representation of what a ruler is doing (in modern terms, press coverage, strategic plans, annual reports, mission statements, spin doctoring, etc.) is more important than reality. Rhetoric creates reality; appearance is more important than action.

A more recent writer, Karl von Clausewitz (1968), a Prussian who wrote explicitly on war in the early nineteenth century has also been influential. In fact, although generally less influential than Machiavelli, he has been more specifically influential on strategists. As Clausewitz (1968: 165) suggests in his book *On War*, strategy 'forms the plan of the war, and to this end it links together the series of acts which are to lead to the final decision, that is to say, it makes the plans for the separate campaigns and regulates the combats to be fought in each'. It is a simple insight that has been at the heart of much of the strategy that has been taught in business schools. Facing competition has been seen to be analogous to facing an enemy in warfare.

The metaphors of war are pervasive. Even a reflective practitioner of strategy, such as Henry Mintzberg, understands strategic positioning as 'consisting of a *launching* device, representing an organization, that sends *projectiles*, namely products and services, at a landscape of *targets*, meaning markets, faced with *rivals*, or competition, in the hope of attaining *fit*' (Mintzberg, 1998: 93). The sources of inspiration could hardly be clearer: strategy, like war, is clearly a very masculine activity. Indeed, the whole notion of competitive strategy is tricked out in ruggedly masculine metaphors, the most notable of which derive from warfare. For instance, there is the case of Stalk and Lachenauer (2004), and the 'hardball manifesto' for strategy that was published in the *Harvard Business Review*. The hardball strategy appears to have some similarities with the neo-con military strategies favoured at that time by the Bush administration. Hardball strategies should be deployed 'in bursts of ruthless intensity' to devastate rivals' profit sanctuaries; competitors' strategies should be 'plagiarized with pride'; the competition should be deceived about the real strategies that the hardball operator is pursuing; massive and overwhelming force should be unleashed, and the objective should be to make the competitor's response too costly by raising competitors' costs. Hardball players, of which Toyota, Dell, and Wal-Mart are singled out, are those who pursue competitive advantage ruthlessly in order to defeat their rivals in the market by doing whatever it takes, while staying, just, on the inside of the law. Although this is an extreme example, it is indicative of a certain kind of macho posturing that is almost *de jure* among the ranks of competitive strategists. Certainly, it is reminiscent of Ullman and Wade's (1996) 'shock and awe' military strategies which were used in 2003 in Operation Iraqi Freedom against Sadam's regime. Indeed, reading their account of what that military strategy entails is eerily reminiscent of a great many strategy texts, including Stalk and Lachenauer (2004). The 'shock and awe' strategy for attaining rapid dominance is introduced by the authors with the following words:

> The basis for Rapid Dominance rests in the ability to affect the will, perception, and understanding of the adversary through imposing sufficient Shock and Awe to achieve the necessary political, strategic, and operational goals of the conflict or crisis that led to the use of force. War, of course, in the broadest sense has been characterized by Clausewitz to include substantial elements of 'fog, friction, and fear.' In the Clausewitzian view, 'shock and awe' were necessary effects arising from application of military power and were aimed at destroying the will of an adversary to resist. Earlier and similar observations had been made by the great Chinese military writer Sun Tzu around 500 BC. Sun Tzu observed that disarming an adversary before battle was joined was the most effective outcome a commander could achieve. Sun Tzu was well aware of the crucial importance of achieving Shock and Awe prior to, during, and in ending battle. He also observed that 'war is deception,' implying that Shock and Awe were greatly leveraged through clever, if not brilliant, employment of force. (Ullman and Wade, 1996)

The ethicality of some of the recommended strategies of deceit, plagiarism and devastation is debatable. However, from the perspective of a commitment to hardball strategies of shock and awe, even to raise ethical questions would be seen as somewhat wimpish, as the mark of being less than a real strategy man. Strategy men (and they are mostly, but not exclusively, men) are hard, tough, fearlessly facing adversaries and devising schemes for their come-uppance. Yet, obviously, strategy is more complex than it first appears to be: it is not just the extension of the arts of war to the sales battles of commerce. For instance, the argot and terminology of strategy has spilled out from its military origins to incorporate the challenges of public service and the altruism of the voluntary organization, for which extreme prejudice may hardly be a viable option. Admittedly, all of these sectors of organizations may be said to require strategies if they are to secure their aims and objectives, but what model of strategist to be or not to be – that is the question. It is also a question of surprisingly recent provenance.

the mundane beginnings of strategy

Strategic management has a short actual history, albeit a pre-history that can be extended back to Chandler, Clausewitz, Machiavelli, or even Sun Tzu, for those who enjoy constructing pedigrees. According to Hambrick and Chen (2008), the beginnings date to the introduction of a course in business policy at Harvard in the 1920s. By March 1970, when ten professors met in Chicago to germinate the seeds of the Business Policy and Planning Division of the American Academy of Management (AoM), the idea of a capstone course in business policy and planning was well established. A social movement had developed around claims to the specific and substantial identity of a phenomenon in which labels, forums, disciples, advocates and publicity all played their part. By 1979 the field had been re-badged as 'strategy' rather than 'business planning' and in 1980 the Strategic Management Society and the *Strategic Management Journal* were established, providing a second string to the strategy bow from that already established in the AoM.

The shift from planning to strategy was due to a complex set of reasons. First, in a free enterprise model, the idea of planning was anathema to those raised on the economics of Friedman or Von Hayek.

Central planning was what socialists did, and did disastrously, and was certainly not something that should be done by captains of industry and top management teams. Second, planning clearly wasn't what it was cracked up to be, as was indicated by the failure of the majority of oil companies' strategists to foresee the consequences of a Middle Eastern war and the formation of the OPEC cartel. Third, and perhaps most significantly, the notion of planning did not suggest a muscular and authoritative frame of reference. It sounded like something that, at worst, communists might do, or, at best, something that the hired help could graph – it certainly was not the preserve of authentic entrepreneurs and certainly wasn't the work of captains of industry. Like generals, they were concerned to conquer the terrain that they operated on and hold it in a dominant position. That competition was war by other means had long been understood. To wage war generals need strategy and captains of industry require it no less. Once strategy was born, then its market was assured – who would want to be caught in the battlefield of commerce with no strategy to speak of?

Differentiation did not stop with the creation of strategy *per se*. It continued with the development of distinct emphases and sub-fields within the general frame of strategy, as we will chart in this book. In part, the rise of these fields can be tied to the creation of a distinctive intellectual capital and kudos by strategic management gurus, such as Porter or Peters. Also, the rise of major international strategy consultancies, all of which needed to differentiate their intellectual property, contributed. It was necessary, in market terms, for McKinsey to be able to differentiate its strategy, products and models from those of the Boston Consulting Group, for example. Institutionally, the championing of a capstone course in the MBA by the American Assembly of Collegiate Schools of Business, together with the pool of ex-executives who graduated with DBAs, meant that there was a cohort of people who could legitimately label themselves 'strategists'.

The field of strategy was constituted by those who affirmed themselves as strategists sharing a sense of being a collective entity, a collective will that was reinforced by the mobilization of resources and the construction of institutional frameworks, such as journals, chairs and courses, enabling adherents to claim legitimacy. Strategic management was political from its inception even when, as we shall see, it often wrote the political out of those organization strategies on which it reflected. It arose as a social movement, and it rapidly evolved into several lagged and overlapping social movements, occurring in recurrent waves, which have been accommodated into the evolving fold, as we will chart in this book. As social movements go, strategy is a very conservative cocktail – take a large slug of pretty boring industrial economics, add a few generous measures of folksy homespun wisdom that reinterprets business success, throw in some hoary war stories concerning the great and the good, stir in a measure of machismo and some showmanship, top it off with a dash of conservative politics and *voila, c'est strategy*!

conclusion

Strategy has claimed many parents. We think that if legitimacy is an issue, then Machiavelli is the best parent to adopt. War has been a matter of strategy far longer than business, so it is not surprising that many early ideas about strategy were framed by warfare. According to a Machiavellian logic, policy follows power. War also demonstrates, in its appalling costs, the ease with which strategic thinking can hang on to outmoded ideas about how to fight. The aphorism that generals usually fight the present war with the lessons learnt from the last war is apt – and nowhere is the aphorism more aptly seen in practice than in the dreadful squandering of human life in the First World War, especially that fateful July day on the Somme about which we have remarked. Yet, as we shall see, there is far more to strategy than just the art of war. And, as Machiavelli realized clearly, the gains of war can sometimes be achieved much more economically through other means. That is the insight that made Clausewitz famous – he argued that war is merely the continuation of politics by other means. Similarly, we might argue that strategy is the continuation of military planning through other means. The end is still the same – to be victorious in the field of battle – it is merely the arena that has shifted. Competition is war by other means and, so the story goes, you need strategy to win it.

2

Planning the Future in Turbulent Environments

An economic historian, Alfred DuPont Chandler, did much to engage academic interest in strategy. Chandler was a business historian who enjoyed access to the archives of some major US businesses, including DuPont, the family business. He looked, in particular, at the creation of a national market in the USA during the nineteenth century, as a result of the growth of the intercontinental railways which replaced separate and distinct regional markets. Chandler's story is quite simple: changes in the environment – the railways as a means of connecting people and goods – created a need for new strategies. To quote him directly:

> Modern business enterprise is the institutional response to the rapid pace of technological innovation and increasing consumer demand in the United States during the second half of the 19th century. (Chandler, 1977: 12)

As new strategies were developed, they required a new organizational structure to house them. Thus, strategy, driven by changes in the environment, should drive the organization. Structure follows strategy. Chandler focused attention on the strategic plan driving, dominating and determining organizational structure. Reflecting on strategies became an inevitable means to success (Chandler, 1962: 15).

Chandler looked at how, in the USA, nineteenth-century preindustrial, small-scale, family-owned and rudimentarily managed enterprises were transformed into large-scale, impersonally owned and bureaucratically managed multi-divisional structures in the twentieth century. Until the advent of the continental railway system in America, business organizations remained typically small, usually under the control of merchants. The first change was due to the enormous geographic diversity of the railways. To manage their geographic spread they developed military models of bureaucracy and a modern 'multi-unit' corporate form. Many of the managers of these entities were drawn from the military academy of West Point which, similarly to the French military academy on which it was based, had a heavy quotient of mathematics and engineering on the syllabus. West Point produced a 'new type of businessman. It is worth emphasizing again that they were salaried employees with little or no financial interest in the companies they served. Moreover most had had specialized training ... [as] civil engineers' (Chandler, 1977: 95).

Keith Hoskin and Richard MacVe (1986, 1988) argue, convincingly, that West Point played a crucial role in developing American management. So what is the story about West Point? Why do Hoskin and MacVe think it is so important in the development of modern strategy? Modelled on the Ecole Polytechnique in Paris, West Point was grammatocentric in that it relied on the act of writing to run an organization, building administrative capacities from these as a set of possibilities for running an organization. Action in the military was delivered by the word written down in despatches; in the bureaucratic firm these despatches became formulated as written instructions to be followed, literally, in routine action. Hoskin and MacVe put Chandler on his head by arguing that the practices developed at West Point gave rise to the modern American firm – rather than such practices being a response to technological and economic developments.

Returning to Chandler's argument, the markets that the railways opened up caused the second change. The possibilities of a mass market could now be entertained. Chandler argued that as businesses enlarged they found it more efficient to incorporate the multiple services previously bought on the market from commission agents, such as the purchase of raw materials, debt financing, marketing and distribution. Administrative coordination began to replace market exchanges as the major mechanism of control because it was technically a more efficient way of doing *a greater volume* of business. Productivity and profits were higher and costs were lower where the fragmentation of markets was replaced with the rudimentary bureaucratization of organization.

The end of the nineteenth century saw a wave of horizontal diversification mergers and vertical mergers incorporating suppliers, marketing outlets and so on. The upshot of these was that what had been distinct family businesses were reconstituted under one centre of organizational control. Past family owners were often retained, now as more or less independent managers in the new organizations fulfilling contracts with labour they hired and organized. Organizations grew as a strategic response to the failure of markets, where contracts tend to be longer- rather than shorter-term, where the environment was more, rather than less, certain, and where the barriers to entry for new agents were high. Implicitly, these barriers were frequently organizational in that they concerned the capacity to hire labour, raise credit and secure supplies. Hence, modern organizational forms were a necessary strategic adjustment to market conditions. Chandler identified the genesis of the M-form as occurring in the late nineteenth century, developing as a means of coordinating ever vaster enterprises. Chandler's work has dominated business history for the last thirty years and it still remains a powerful explanation of the emergence of modern strategy. Perhaps, Hoskin et al. (2006) argue, the M-form actually came into existence seventy years previously with the expansion of the Pennsylvania Railroad company.

In Chandler's model, strategy is the result of smart decisions that achieve a fit between market opportunities and structure. If early strategy was largely a question of individuals being smart, by the latter half of the twentieth century smart individuals had smart machines to assist them further. For as long as strategy had to function with the resources of the human mind, it remained limited to what its strategic thinkers could process. Of course, computers – to the extent that they can deal with binary representations of data – can handle far more data than a strategic thinker, and do so far faster. So, computer technology gave hope to planners that one day they would be able to analyze past data to determine the future probabilities for an organization.

Chandler is an example of how analysis creates a new conceptual object – the strategic plan that drives, dominates and determines organizational structure. Reflecting on strategies became an inevitable means to success 'in response to the opportunities and needs created by changing population and changing national income and by technological innovation' (Chandler, 1962: 15). Put simply, changes in the environment create a need for new strategies, a theme endlessly repeated by contingency theory. As a consequence, these new strategies require a new organizational structure (note the functional language of needs). In both steps, the organization reacts passively: it is a passive victim of environmental changes to which it responds through developing adequate strategies. Strategy, again, is a reaction to which structure then reacts. Structure follows strategy and strategy is driven by environmental changes. The chain of cause and effect is linear, simple and trivial, but nonetheless decisive: 'Unless structure follows strategy, inefficiency rules' (Chandler, 1962: 314).

A whole range of arguments seek to justify this hierarchy: management must plan in order to coordinate an organization's activities; to ensure that the future is taken into account; to be rational, and to control (Mintzberg, 1994: 16–19). Thus, strategy, and strategic planning especially, can be seen as an example of what Nietzsche (1968) analyzed as the 'will to power' – the will to control, predict and dominate the future. As he argued, plans are one of the most effective and common devices used to try to exercise power over things and people. The plan is a means 'which can eliminate and incorporate uncertainty' (Tsivacou, 1996: 70; see also Kallinikos, 1996; Kallinikos and Cooper, 1996). It is meant to predict the future and thus render the incalculable tomorrow into a predictable and thus controllable pattern. The plan as a modern form of rationality began to turn into a steel-hardened frame as the metaphors of strategy were further developed into the rational planning model.

Igor Ansoff: the rational planning model

The Strategic Planning School was based on the analysis of large amounts of data for long-range planning and rational decision-making, extrapolating from the past to plan the future. The most important contribution to the Planning School was Igor Ansoff's book, *Corporate Strategy* (1965). Ansoff was an engineer and mathematician who served in the US Naval Reserve in the Second World War and, using his Russian background, liaised for the USA with the Russian Navy during the war.

Ansoff identified three different levels of action:

- Administrative action
- Operational action
- Strategic action.

Whereas the first level (administrative) concerned direct production processes, the second level (operational) focused on the maximization of efficiency of the first-level processes. The realm of strategic action is directed towards an organization's relation with its environment, especially as this involves forecasting strategic turbulence. Such forecasting looks at likely changes in the environment. Planning adequate responses and controlling the organization's correct realization of these plans should be top management's task. He advocated a classic *rational planning approach* to strategy. It was to have a strong influence in areas such as project management in the construction industry and large-scale engineering and exploration projects in the oil industry. It contributed directly to the canon of the project management body of knowledge. In this respect it follows on from the direction that F.W. Taylor set at the birth of management. Ansoff's influence is echoed in modern management thinking that understands those at the top as the strategic thinkers of an organization, seeing their task as defining the big picture, steering the organization with a strong grasp, whereas the lower levels of the hierarchy realize and implement what they have been told but which they could never see – because they are outside the corporate elites who set the strategic vision.

Ansoff's product/mission matrix is particularly well known to business school students. It represents an early attempt to encompass all you need to know in a simple 2×2 matrix. The matrix has two sides to it: one is labelled *markets* and the other *products*. Both products and markets can be dichotomously conceived as 'current' or 'new'. It yields the picture shown in Figure 2.1.

Market penetration strategies seek to sell more existing products or services into current markets. You do this by targeting existing customers to buy more by offering deals such as volume discounts, enrolling customers into special bonus card and customer relationship management schemes. When increased volumes of existing product

Product Market	Existing	New
Existing	Market Penetration	Product Development
New	Market Development	Diversification

Figure 2.1   Ansoff's matrix

can be shipped to existing customers, then economies of scale can be achieved. Such economies occur through larger volume manufacturing, the distribution of a greater amount of product through the existing channels, enhanced purchasing power for increased bulk materials at lower rates, and a higher amount of output to allay fixed overhead costs. Large computer manufacturers such as Dell or Hewlett-Packard would be good examples of this.

Market development strategies seek to sell more of the same products or services into new markets. New markets are developed by defeating the competition in existing markets or opening up new markets, often in new countries, for existing products. Many western universities have sought to 'sell' MBA degrees to students in different parts of the world. In many cases this has been through distance learning, so students don't even need to attend the university! One strategy widely used here is to build a brand name and extend it into allied markets, much as Virgin has done as a lifestyle brand, in travel, mobile phones, colas and so on. New markets do not just have to be in new geographic regions; they may be new functional markets, such as when Apple moved from computers to MP3 players.

Product development strategies are based on trying to sell new products or services into current markets. Think of the way that, when you buy a car, there is plenty of opportunity to buy other branded goods: Porsche bikes, BMW clothes and glasses, Ferrari phones, and so on. Or when you take out a home loan the bank may try to cross-sell you home, contents and life insurance at the same time as you take out the loan.

Diversification strategies are premised on selling new products or services in new markets. Diversification can be approached in four ways:

1   *Horizontal diversification*, when the company acquires or develops new products that could appeal to its current customer groups even though those new products may be technologically unrelated to the existing product lines.
2   *Vertical diversification*, when the company moves into the business of its suppliers or into the business of its customers.
3   *Concentric diversification*, when new product lines or services that have technological and/or marketing synergies with existing product lines are developed, even though the products may appeal to a new customer group.
4   *Conglomerate diversification* often arrived at by accident, as a result of mergers and acquisitions. Sometimes unrelated businesses can be an insurance against the fluctuations of the business cycle in particular branches of business. In some countries, such as Korea, and in Chinese family businesses, unrelated conglomerate portfolios are the normal business model, although they tend to be frowned upon in current western thinking.

sexing up strategy

Well, the account thus far is all well and good, but it is all so … *rational*. Management makes decisions on strategic directions, designs action plans to implement them, and deploys forms of control to evaluate their effects. Usually, the model of decision-making is described as a perfectly well-organized, rational and logical process. First, the problem is defined. Second, all the relevant information that leads to an optimal solution is collected. Third, reviewing the data, management (perhaps with the help of technocratic 'experts') develops several possible solutions. Fourth, evaluating the possible solutions carefully, management makes a decision regarding the optimal solution. Fifth, this solution is implemented in a top-down approach and evaluated constantly by management. Such constant processes of rational decision-making, supported by the latest IT equipment and an army of analysts and consultants, are meant constantly and incrementally to refine and improve an organization's processes and products. Decision-making is discussed as if it were a highly rational activity, where a decision is a rational choice based on a logical connection between cause and effect, made in the context of a rational search for solutions to something defined as a problem, for which the options can be rationally weighted and compared and the optimum decision chosen. Unfortunately, such 'rational actors' are rarely to be found outside introductory textbooks, especially of economics; real life is a bit more complicated.

One of the earliest writers to recognize this complexity was the Nobel Economics laureate, Herbert Simon (1945), who recognized that few, if any, decisions are made under conditions of perfect rationality. Issues are frequently ambiguous, information about alternatives will often be incomplete, and the choice criteria unclear. In addition, others may see the issues, alternatives and choices in utterly different – sometimes antagonistic – terms. And the time, energy and political will to reconcile different positions may well be lacking. Consequently, most decision-making uses criteria that aim for 'satisficing' rather than 'maximizing' utility. Simon developed the term *satsificing* as a mix of to 'satisfy' and to 'suffice': we don't strive to make optimal decisions but decisions that satisfy us and that 'do the trick'. Thus, most decisions are not ideal but make do with what is seen to be available and relevant. Managers operate with 'bounded rationality' rather than complete rationality. Decision-makers can only review a limited range of factors and possibilities in making decisions because of the limitations both of the information available to them and their cognitive and temporal ability to handle its complexity. Hence, they can only ever exercise rationality within the limits of the information available and their ability to make sense of it. Think of how you make decisions on your future career: do you really evaluate all potential future careers you could make? Most of us – including Chris, Stewart, and Martin – have applied a more *satsificing* approach where chance encounters with people open up opportunities that presented themselves as good enough to be explored further. Put simply, decision-making is more improvised than assumed by the rational approach.

Simon makes a contrast between two types of decision that managers may have to deal with. Programmed decisions can be made by reference to existing rubrics (Simon, 1960). The programmed decisions are fairly easy and can be categorized as operational to make solutions by applying organizational rules that subordinates can be trained to follow. Non-programmed decisions have no precedents, are unfamiliar, novel and complex, and cannot be left to subordinates: they are what are sometimes referred to as messy or intractable problems. As Susan Miller and Dave Wilson (2006: 470) put it, topics for decision may be complex, definitions problematic, information unavailable and/or difficult to collect, solutions hard to recognize, and the process generative not so much of solutions as headaches from further problems. Most significant organizational issues involving major commitments of resources that top management teams have to deal with usually fall into this category. Problemistic search, incremental solution, and dynamic non-linear reiteration and redefinition of almost all the terms in the decision mix will characterize these types of activity (Braybrooke and Lindblom, 1963; Lindblom, 1959; Quinn, 1978, 1980).

Incremental decision search and solution means many small steps, which are easier to retrace if things don't go as hoped. 'Once each small step has been taken it gives a clearer picture of what has to be done and the future becomes more focused', as Miller and Wilson (2006: 470) put it. Also, small steps are more likely to cool out resistance than big sweeping changes which will always seem obviously threatening to existing interests in a way that a smaller change – as a part of a larger iterative, emergent and unfolding design – will not. Muddling through, as Lindblom (1959) calls it, is less scary. Common processes in muddling through include finding an initial simple impasse and further investigating it to reveal more complex political issues, from which a basic search for a solution ensues. The search is modified as the complexity and politicality of the issue starts to become more apparent. Next, a basic design for a solution is advanced and then, typically, the basic design is subject to blocking moves from other interests. Finally, a dynamic design process is developed as changes are made, opponents are brought on side, isolated or otherwise neutralized (Mintzberg et al., 1976; Nutt, 1984).

Cohen, March, and Olsen (1972) pushed March and Simon's critique one step further, announcing that the decision-making process in organizations is organized according to the logic of what they call the 'garbage can'. The garbage can refers to situations characterized by 'problematic preferences', 'unclear technology' and 'fluid participation'. The garbage can, of course, is a metaphor. Problems, solutions and decision-makers, unlike in traditional decision theory, are seen to be disconnected. Specific decisions do not follow an orderly process from problem to solution, but are outcomes of several relatively independent streams of events within the organization. Decisions are made when solutions, problems, participants and choices flow around and coincide at a certain point. Like garbage in a can, these adjacencies are often purely random. Yesterday's papers end up stuck to today's rubbish just as downsizing attaches itself to profit forecasts.

William Starbuck (1983) similarly argued that organizations are not so much problem solvers as action generators. Instead of analyzing and deciding rationally how to solve problems, organizations spend most of their time generating problems to which they already have the solutions. It's much more economical that way. They know how to do what they will do, so all they have to do is work out why they will do it. Just think of any consulting business – its solutions to whatever problems occur will be what it currently offers. Products such as total quality management (TQM), business process reengineering (BPR), and so on are solutions to almost every problem, and thus it is not so much the problem that drives the solution but the solution already at hand that is waiting to be applied to a variety of different issues.

Where decisions begin and end, as well as the steps they go through, are not at all as clear as rational models might suggest (Hickson et al., 1986). Hickson and his colleagues looked at 150 decisions in 30 organizations. Some decisions that the organizations' top managers defined as strategic were found to be resolved within a month while others dragged out over four years, with the mean time for strategic decision-making proving to be just over twelve months. Nonetheless, how the decisions were arrived at varied between three predominant processual paths, characterized by *sporadic*, *fluid* and *constricted decision-making*. The more political the matter for decision, the more stakeholders tend to be engaged; the more complex the problems are, the more fluid the processes tend to be. The key stakeholders are usually intra-organizational, typically production, sales and marketing, and accounting in the organizations that were studied.

With regard to the implementation of the decisions made, subsequent research by Hickson et al. (2003) has found that there are two typical ways of managing implementation. Where they have a pretty clear idea of what they are doing, and the likely reactions of others to it, a more planned mode of implementation occurs, based on experience. Where the management team doing the implementation has less experience and is not so sure what they are doing, the receptivity of the context in which the decision is being implemented is crucial. In other words, it matters a great deal if they can succeed in getting key people 'on-side' (Hickson et al., 2003; Miller et al., 2004).

It is one thing to make a decision and quite another to see it through into successful implementation. There are three different ways of connecting decision-making and implementation.

1   *Continuous connectedness* is provided by the involvement of key personnel usually drawn from production, finance and marketing, throughout the processes of decision-making and implementation. They see the whole phased process through, provide a memory and retain commitment, as other interested parties drop out of the loop.
2   *Causal connectedness* is more complex. Three elements are crucial: the degree of contention, seriousness and endurance of the processes of decision and implementation. High degrees of contention tend to limit familiar solutions – these are clearly not working if the contention is high – and they also indicate a context less receptive to whatever solution is being proposed. Contentious decisions tend to be faster, perhaps because under these circumstances management decides to crash through or crash. Decisions characterized by a high degree of consensus take longer to make and implement, but there may well be a lot less firefighting afterwards (Dooley et al., 2000). The more serious and important the decision being made, in terms of the top management team's opinion, the more specific will be the steps taken

to implement it in an experience-based approach, while, from a readiness-based approach, a greater priority will be given to implementation. There is also a relationship between how long the consequences of the decision are expected to endure (endurance) and acceptability. The longer-lasting the implications of the decision will be, the more the top management team should care about the acceptability of what is being implemented. Crashing through under these circumstances will more likely lead to a crash than a successful decision, especially where the key buy-in of production, finance and marketing has not been achieved – where the process has low acceptability.

3   *Anticipatory connectedness*, involving thinking forward in terms of the future perfect tense – what will we have achieved when we have implemented the decisions we will have made – is important for decision-makers. If we do implement this decision, what will be the effect? Thinking in an anticipatory way about the impact of the decision can feed back on the decision itself. If implementation of the posited and projected decision seems unlikely to be smooth, because implementation will be intricate, then the decision-making process probably needs revisiting, thus dragging out the process further. There is a form of feedback from imagined implementation to possible decision, making the decision process more protracted.

At the core of all these sexed-up accounts of what rational planning strategy might be is a concern with the uses of power – by those implementing decisions as well as by those resisting what is implied by these decisions. And this brings us back to Machiavelli: policy does follow power.

Rational planners, on the whole, have not handled power rationally. The assumption is that strategists formulate policies and the top management team decides on the implementation of the strategy. Friedmann (1998: 29) argues that the 'biggest problem' in rational planning is ambivalence about power. Ambivalence is perhaps a tad generous; planning has, by and large, ignored power. Planning's neglected face is power. One writer who has recognized this is Flyvbjerg (2002), in the context of urban planning – but his points apply equally well to the use of the rational planning model in strategy.

The space between the rational plan and power is under-investigated in at least two directions. First, there is little accounting for how the limits to rationality are framed by a bounded rationality that implies power. Certain assumptions are made tacitly, and certain other assumptions are never challenged explicitly because of the power vested in maintaining these assumptions. For instance, in the 1980s, the Fleet Street print unions, through their local 'Chapels', as their branches were known, had enormous sway over what newspaper proprietors could and could not do because of restrictive union agreements and arrangements. However, by the mid-1980s the stranglehold that the print unions had exercised could now be by-passed technologically due to innovations in printing technology. Yet, until the decision was made by Rupert Murdoch in 1986 to move production of *The Times*, *The Sun* and *The News of the World* from Fleet Street to Wapping, in the newly developed Docklands area, the proprietors had not acted strategically to by-pass restrictive practices and use the new technologies. The proprietors had not dared to face down the power of the print unions. So, as the example shows, power enters into the formulation of planning, of constituting what can and cannot be done. And of course, given the lock-out and picketing that lasted for over a year, as the unions demonstrated, power also enters into the implementation of rational planning.

Machiavelli, our model for the origins of strategy, understood these points well. For him, the use of power was the essence of strategy. Flyvbjerg (2002: 355–6) sees himself as a modern Machiavelli; not surprisingly, power is the heart of his account of rational planning. Following his lead, we suggest that at the core of any strategy exercise are four key questions.

1   Where is planning taking the organization? By asking this question we should be focusing on what futures we want to be in – if we do this, what, in all probability, is likely to happen? What resistance will be likely, what counter-strategies will be required? Do we have the will, the resolve and the resources to stick with the direction?

2   Who gains and who loses, and by which mechanisms of power? Who within the organization will benefit from the strategy planned? Who within the organization is likely to lose? How are they likely to respond if their analysis matches that of the strategists? How disposable are these people? How essential are they? What deals will need to be done?

3   Is what is planned desirable in terms of larger strategic considerations in addition to those of immediate shareholder value? What about the

broader set of stakeholders, such as customers, NGOs, community and civic organizations, or authoritative leaders in politics and the community?

4   After taking all these considerations into account, what should be done?

Flyvbjerg's (2002) analysis of the relation between rationality and power shows that while power produces rationality (because power delimits the bounds of reason, of what is and is not possible), rationality does not produce power so much as rationalizations of power. Power is asymmetrical in its relation to rationality because power tends to dominate, determine and frame what is taken to be rational. What is taken to be rational does not have the same impact on extant power relations where it points to their suppression or transformation. That is why matters of rational planning are always matters of power relations, even when the reality of power is buried by the rhetoric of rationality.

conclusion

The assumptions of rational planning remain the most influential in the field, despite the assaults on them by bounded rationality, garbage cans and power perspectives. In many ways this is because the plan becomes a document that is tangible, identifying what is to be done and where it will take the organization, a plan that becomes institutionalized in the fabric of the organization. Sticking to the plan, proceeding according to the plan and doing what the plan says all become the micro-politics of power's disciplines. The plan, by virtue of becoming an object that is reified, that is made concrete and attributed powers, becomes the very instrument through which the organization's rationality is imposed. Along with this rationality, the plan spews forth rationalizations of and for action, it frames organizational actions and relations, it shapes power in the interstices of the organization. Plans are powerful, but you would never learn that from reading most accounts of rational planning in strategy.

3

Strategy = Understanding What's Outside the Firm

███████ Porter, economics and industry analysis

Doubtlessly, the most influential strategy theorist at the end of the twentieth century was Michael Porter, the Bishop William Lawrence University Professor at Harvard Business School. Michael Porter's academic background is in the field of industrial economics and most of his work bears the unmistakable imprint of his training. In each case, Porter's work was based on readily accepted industrial economics concepts that, when translated into business schools, became new and innovative concepts. In this regard, it is difficult to overstate the influence of Porter on the canon of strategic management. Not surprisingly, then, Porter's key message to the business world was simple: the potential of an organization is determined by the structure of the industry and the market it is operating in.

Such an insight might be characterized as an outside-in approach to strategy. With this mode of thinking, the task of strategy is to understand and exploit industry weaknesses and opportunities. Put simply, the fact that some firms are consistently more profitable than others cannot be explained through their strategic choices; rather, it is the attractiveness of the industry that determines profitability. If you are in the airline business right now (June 2007), then you would find it very hard to develop a profitable strategy. The entire industry is losing billions of dollars year by year so your strategic initiatives might not be able to change the tide. Looking at the pharmaceutical industry, the picture changes dramatically. Pharmaceutical companies enjoy over-average 20 per cent profits, not because of superior firm-level strategies but because of industry and market characteristics.

Drugs are bought by large hospitals that are less cost-conscious, the barriers to entry are extremely high (because the cost of R&D is prohibitive for any new entrant to the market), and so on. These industry characteristics allow profitable pharmaceutical giants to grow. Porter's theory focuses on the industry characteristics that enable firms to grow. In a nutshell, the industry structure sets the limits for what individual firms can (and cannot) do.

strategic differentiation

The arenas in which competitive strategy occurs usually involve quality or performance of product, cost and price, sales promotion and service, and the strength of sales channels. Typically, these four arenas for strategic differentiation can lead to three distinct organizational strategies. But not always!

Where firms do have a sense of themselves as being involved in a competitive environment they will need to pose a number of basic strategic questions:

1 *Product differentiation.* Companies such as Coca-Cola or Nike invest a great deal of time and money to brand their products and position them uniquely in the marketplace. Any competitor will struggle with the distinctiveness and the uniqueness that these products represent in the (potential) client's eyes.

2 *Market segmentation.* Due to demographic factors (age, income, etc.), socio-economic factors (social class, etc.), geographic factors (climate, regional culture, etc.), cultural factors (tastes, taboos and preferences, such as the Chinese preference for red as a lucky colour, etc.) and psychological factors (lifestyle, etc.) different customers have different needs. Segmenting the market into competitively relevant groups allows you to tailor products and their marketing to one precise group of (potential) customers. For instance, fashion retailers target particular markets. In the UK, retailer's such as Primark and New Look target the teenage market, Zara targets the late teen and twenty-something 'fast fashion' market, whereas firms like Karen Millen target the affluent 'aspirational' market composed mainly of professionals from their mid to late twenties onwards. Firms like Oasis are currently trying to reposition themselves higher in the market, alongside brands such as Reiss.

3   *Price policy and cost leadership*. Own brands in supermarkets build
    on this strategy. Offering comparable products for a cheaper price
    is a simple but successful strategy, as long as you operate according
    to the economics of scale, which means increasing the quantity of
    the product so that the cost per unit decreases. The large UK super-
    market chains, such as Tesco and Sainsbury's, have colossal buying
    power, to such an extent that for many products they are able to sell
    them at a lower retail price than a smaller store could actually buy
    them for.

While the centrality of these three points is unlikely to be disputed
today, they were not quite so evident when strategy first emerged as
an area of academic concern. The reason for this was that the earliest school to emerge with an interest in strategy was one that had a
strong economic history focus: it sought to establish why the companies that had succeeded in the twentieth century had been able to do
so, and what their evolutionary path had been.

strategy means positioning oneself in a competitive environment

The *Positioning School* was strongly shaped and influenced by
Michael Porter's *Competitive Strategy: Techniques for Analyzing
Industries and Competitors* (1980). As the subtitle of his book indicates, Porter focused on the structure of industries and their impact
on strategies. Porter developed analytical tools to understand more
differentiated environments and provided a more refined way of
understanding and managing strategy. Porter elaborated that the
determinants of an organization's profit can be summarized through
his Five Forces Model (Figure 3.1).

Porter argues that the profitability of an organization depends on the
bargaining power it exercises in negotiating prices with suppliers and
customers. Logically, a strong bargaining position means that an organization pays (relative to its competitors) less to its suppliers and is
capable of selling with a higher profit margin to customers. The economic structure of the market – represented in the five forces – determines the bargaining power of enterprises. For example, in a market

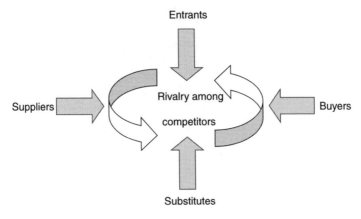

Figure 3.1   Porter's Five Forces Model

with low barriers to entry, the threat of newly competing rivals is high only when the level of profitability in this industry is high as well. Thus, a strategy for a company in an industry with a high threat of new entrants might be to choose the strategy of 'limit pricing', meaning that it will keep its profit low in order to avoid attracting competitors.

According to Porter, the threat of substitutes also influences the bargaining power of companies. Whereas companies that offer similar or identical products or services are rivals (two ski resorts, for instance), substitution means products or services that are not in direct competition but have nonetheless an important impact (e.g. a holiday provider offering attractive packages to spend winter holidays under palm trees in the Caribbean at a classy resort as an alternative to skiing at Cloisters). Strategic management, in Porter's sense, means navigating through the web of opportunities and threats framed by external competitive forces.

the value chain

In 1985 Porter came up with a second major contribution to the field of strategic management: *Competitive Advantage: Creating and Sustaining Superior Performance*, which shifted attention towards

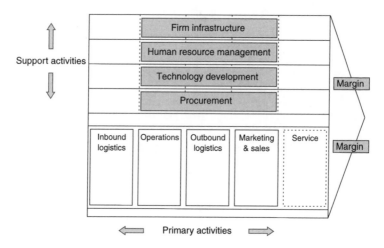

Figure 3.2   Porter's concept of the value chain

internal dimensions of strategic management. Porter again embedded strategy within the market forces characteristic of an industry. It was here that he developed the concept of the value chain to analyze processes of production or delivery of services (see Figure 3.2). While an industry is characterized by the process of transforming resources and/or raw materials into final products or services, the concept of the industry value chain analyzes the steps in this process that actually add value to these services and products. The added value is the difference between cost of production and the revenues realized in the market-place. That sounds more awkward than it actually is. Think of a pre-ferred restaurant that serves the most enjoyable food. It transforms fresh produce into great meals. However, the value it adds consists of the skills of the chef, the friendliness of the waiter, and the overall ambience. In short, the added value is that which exceeds the value of the sum of the parts. Sometimes the value added is quite surprising!

There are several primary activities (from inbound logistics to ser-vices) that describe the chain of production. Porter also includes sup-port activities that keep the primary activities going. Analytically, the model investigates the value that specific parts of an organization add to its services or products.

What does the value chain concept add to our example of the restaurant? Through analyzing the value chain, the manager might find out that it is worth spending more time and money on buying better quality food if, as a result, the restaurant could increase its prices and its turnover. In order to spend more time and money on shopping, management might decide to cancel the pianist who currently plays in the restaurant each night, having decided, through some basic market research, that guests came not because but in spite of her: thus she did not add any value to the chain and, subsequently, is terminated.

Outsourcing often flows from a value chain analysis. Outsourcing means eliminating parts of the production system that do not add value to the product and that can be better or more cheaply contracted ('outsourced') to another company that is a specialist in this area. For instance, instead of having their own accountancy department, companies might outsource the tasks to specialists who can do it better and more cheaply, thus preserving more value, than if it were internally organized.

Outsourcing usually involves either going to specialist firms that can provide a non-core service or element of production more cheaply, such as IT or HRM services, or it can involve seeking out a supplier of core elements who can deliver at a much cheaper price than the company could itself. Often this means taking advantage of the huge disparities in cost structures that prevail in the global economy. The initial decision to move from an in-house service to an outsourcing provider is major. In the vast majority of cases, when organizations move a business function from intra-organizational to third-party control, significant efficiency gains are expected by focusing 'time, effort and capital on value-creating activities that yield a competitive advantage, an improved overall performance, and security for the organizations' long-term survival' (Hunter and Cooksey, 2004: 27).

Outsourcing is not a new phenomenon: in major production industries such as automotives, the outsourcing of initially non-core and latterly core functions and services has been progressively used since the 1930s (Macaulay, 1966). However, services outsourcing, although common for some time in specialist areas such as advertising and legal services, increased dramatically from the mid-1990s and it is now one of the growth areas for management consultancy firms. The outsourcing of sectors such as IT and telecommunications and business processing occurred with the dawning of advanced digital telecommunications services that facilitated the availability of this option. The imperative to outsource – as distinct from the opportunity to do so – was a result of other dynamics of the digital age, primarily globalization and increased competition, leading to a continual need to improve efficiency from productivity and to increase service levels. Thus, vertically integrated services were no longer seen as the best organizational arrangements for gaining competitive advantage.

The Competitive Advantage of Nations: Porter's diamond.

In his relentless pursuit to differentiate himself strategically, Porter (1990) has turned his attention to questions of competitive strategy at the national level. Commissioned by former US President, Ronald Reagan, in the 1980s, Porter led a multinational team of researchers who conducted a comprehensive study of 12 nations to learn what leads to success. The genesis of the study was the American government's increasing disquiet at the rise of Japanese economic power, which, *inter alia*, saw North American consumer electronics and car companies lose out to their Japanese competitors. The loss of competitiveness was especially traumatic, as North America had enjoyed unparalleled cultural and economic dominance in the post-Second World War period. Some commentators referred to this as the age of *Pax Americana*.

Reagan's brief to Porter was to search for the elixir of success and find out what had gone wrong. How could America be competitive once again? Porter started out by rephrasing the question, arguing that talking in terms of national competitiveness is a problematic activity, as it is an exercise that conflates and aggregates different sectors and regions. For instance, in the 1970s and 1980s Britain lost competitiveness in a number of sectors, such as car production and consumer electronics; in others, such as confectionary, financial services and military arms, it retained competitiveness. Taking the point more literally, at the time of the UK's economic nadir, container loads of Hobnobs (an English biscuit) were being routinely exported to Japan!

Porter not only stresses the importance of the sector but also concentrates attention on the region. For instance, in a relatively small country such as Britain, there are stark differences between different regions. Porter's study looked at 20 sectors, across 12 nations at three points in time. His research question was whether the homebase of a firm matters? Porter suggests that the homebase – where your organization starts out – is of critical importance. The implication of this is that a firm such as Benetton, a very Italian story, could not have succeeded in the same way had it started up elsewhere. Equally, think how particular genres of music have been so tightly associated with particular cities. What is it about Manchester in England that has led to so many bands – Joy Division, The Smiths, Stone Roses, Happy Mondays and Oasis, to name a few – emerging from there? Clearly, a key role was played by Tony Wilson, a TV presenter who became the owner of a nightclub, the Hacienda, and a record label, Factory Records, which created a small industry of venues, records and bookings based around the Manchester music scene. Or what was it about Seattle that led to it being the homebase for the enormously successful 'grunge' scene? Why have countries such as France and Germany been so lamentably poor at producing competent pop and rock music? Why is it that so much movie-making takes place in Hollywood, Bollywood or Hong Kong? These examples illustrate Porter's point: homebase matters. Perhaps this seems paradoxical, given that many celebrants of globalization emphasize precisely the opposite point, that homebase is immaterial in an age where the tyrannies of time and space have collapsed. Yet, consider the most ubiquitous industry of the global era: the design and production of digital software. It is centred on key locales such as Microsoft in Seattle or Apple in Cupertino, even if the iPod you are listening to is manufactured in China.

In exploring Porter's diamond, our position is that it is a useful framework to think with but you should not accept it without qualification. Moreover, such is the power of Porter's brand – governments employ him, corporate executives listen to him, students study him – that his nostrums can become self-fulfilling. Having sounded that caveat, let us

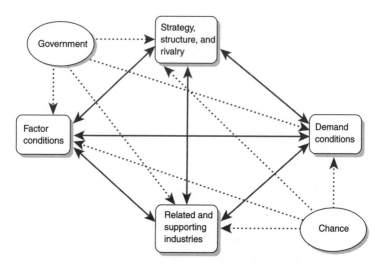

Figure 3.3   Porter's diamond

explore Porter's diamond. The diamond is a constellation of four primary components: (1) strategy, structure and rivalry; (2) demand conditions; (3) factor conditions; and (4) related and supporting industries – and two secondary components (chance and government) (see Figure 3.3).

The major determinants in Porter's diamond are the following conditions, as they are shaped by government policies and chance:

1 Factor conditions (i.e. the nation's position in factors of production, such as skilled labour and infrastructure).
2 Demand conditions (i.e. sophisticated customers in home market).
3 Related and supporting industries.
4 Firm strategy, structure and rivalry (i.e. conditions for the organization of companies and the nature of domestic rivalry).
5 Government (i.e. the state providing stable economic conditions with fiscal and monetary policy that encourages enterprise).
6 Chance (i.e. the role of serendipity and unintended consequences).

factor conditions

Porter outlines what he takes to be crucial important factor conditions. In a departure from classical economics, Porter downplays natural endowments such as land, raw materials and so forth. Natural endowments refer to factors of production such as labour, land, natural resources, capital and infrastructure. He argues that in advanced capitalism created factors are more important. Created factors include specialized factors, such as education, transport infrastructure and health services. For instance, when looking at America after the Second World War, Porter makes the point that education levels were comparatively high. This was in no small part due to the 'GI Bill', which provided free college places for those who had served in the US forces. Porter looks into the research and knowledge-creating capabilities of a homebase. For instance, he would regard institutes that generate specific knowledge (such as the Australian Institute of Sports) as being the means that can lead to a homebase being relatively more competitive. Many 'New World' wine producers have specific wine research institutes creating knowledge that in turn can be fed back into the innovation process.

Porter argues that a lack of resources can actually help countries to become competitive because abundance generates waste while scarcity generates an innovative mindset. Countries that have scarce resources are forced to innovate to overcome their shortage: Japan is the most often cited example of a country with no natural resources. Equally, the Netherlands is a world leader in the production of tomatoes and flowers, although its climate is hardly suited to either pursuit, with much being grown under glass. It did have pre-eminence in the tulip market in the seventeenth century when the tulip market was a national obsession and an inflationary bubble, rather like the dotcom market before the 2001 crash. Its competitive advantage in flowers dates from this period (see Moggach, 2000, whose novel, *Tulip Fever*, is an evocative and romantic rendering of that period in history). The Netherlands is also a world leader in hydraulic science and civil engineering, which is less surprising because so much of its land is actually reclaimed and below sea level. It is an expertise that they have had to develop to survive, but is also one that Dutch companies have been able to market worldwide, especially in small states such as Singapore, for whom reclamation is the only option for growth. Japan, the southern Chinese cities of Hong Kong and Macau as well as the city-state of Singapore, are all places where habitable and usable land is in short supply and all are famous for their efforts at land reclamation, often using Dutch expertise.

■■■■■■ demand

Porter argues that a sophisticated domestic market is an important element in producing competitiveness. Porter's interest is in the number of independent buyers in a market – something that meant that he immediately wrote off the consumers in the Soviet Bloc, which was still in existence while he was writing the book. However, it was not just in the Eastern bloc that consumer choice was limited. For instance, even in western economies such as the UK, certain markets were relatively protected. British firms in the market for company cars in the UK often insisted that their people had to choose a British car: for the average salesperson this meant a choice between British Leyland, Ford or Vauxhall automobiles. The market for these 'salesmen's [sic] cars' was, to a large extent, captive. Captive markets do not drive innovation.

When the market is open and competitive, then demands for high quality will come from the close proximity of demanding consumers, which requires successful firms to be smarter and more innovative. Customers who will complain and not be afraid to switch their loyalties if service is unsatisfactory help make better products and processes. Some have argued that this has been a particular problem in some cultures, such as Britain, where people tend not to make a fuss or complain. This would probably do much to explain the relatively poor levels of service, experienced, for instance, in restaurants and hotels. Indeed, it has been noted (Clark, 2000; Whipp and Clark, 1986) that one of the real problems that the British car company Rover faced, before its eventual dismemberment, was that people did not complain when their new car had several minor problems. Rather than complain, many British customers would simply do the repairs themselves. It was a lack of assertiveness that cost Rover dear as it tried to establish itself on the world stage. For instance, in many overseas markets, buying a British car became widely regarded as a passport to rapid depreciation and unreliable performance. A good friend would counsel against it. Now of course firms such as Rover belong to the history books, with various attempts to revive the firm having failed. Rover is a poignant instance of poor strategy-making having calamitous effects for the workforce and surrounding locale of Longbridge, in South Birmingham.

Where a nation's discriminating values spread to other countries, then local firms will become competitive in the global market. One example is the Australian wine industry, which has become the preferred provider of wine in many key European markets, beating the French at their own game, due to offering quality, innovation and value. Equally, consider the consumer electronics market, which has been dominated by the Japanese for the past few decades. In the 1970s, the bigger the stereo, generally the better it was likely to be. Any self-respecting 70s student had speakers that covered a whole wall – the better to listen to Pink Floyd or Led Zeppelin. By comparison, contemporary stereos are tiny. These changes have been driven by consumer demand in Japan. Japan is a densely populated country with serious shortages of space for real estate. The corollary of this is that it serves to fuel demand for smaller products. Thus the innovations made in consumer electronics, which saw products become ever smaller, arose from the Japanese predilection for 'smaller is better'. This was combined with a very active consumer market, one that bought new products such as cameras, stereos, and walkmans with great regularity. The key for Porter is, therefore, the extent to which home demand shapes, or at least reflects, world demand.

related and supporting industries

Strongly related and supporting industries are important to the competitiveness of firms, including supplier and related industries. Think of sub-national areas such as Milan, for fashion goods, or Silicon Valley for software. Clustering close to competitors enables easier knowledge diffusion, a pool of more knowledgeable employees, consumers' association of a region with a product and high quality and, therefore, some market power. When there is a large industry presence in an area, it will increase the supply of specific factors, such as workers with industry-specific training, since they will tend to get higher returns and have more chances of better employment. At the same time, upstream firms that supply intermediate inputs will invest there to save on transport costs, tariffs, inter-firm communication costs, and inventories. Downstream firms who use the industry product as an input will also invest in the area, causing additional savings. Related industries that use similar inputs or whose goods are purchased by the same set of customers will also invest, triggering subsequent rounds of investment and virtuous growth cycles.

firm structure, strategy and rivalry

Domestic capital markets affect firm strategies: some markets have a long-term outlook while others are focused on the short term. Countries with a short-term outlook (such as the USA, where performance on markets is highly dependent on quarterly reporting) tend to be more competitive in industries with short-term investment cycles, such as the computer industry. Countries with a long-term outlook will tend to be more competitive in industries where investment is long term, such as the pharmaceutical industry in Switzerland. A country will be competitive in an industry whose key personnel hold positions that are considered prestigious and intense competition spurs innovation. Domestic rivalry for final goods stimulates the emergence of an industry that provides specialized intermediate goods. Keen domestic competition leads to more sophisticated consumers who come to expect upgrading and innovation. Thus, the diamond promotes clustering. Michael Porter argues that the more competition in the homebase the better, the rationale being that it is smart for a company to locate itself in a homebase where there is fierce competition.

government

Forming the inner part of the diamond, the above four points are supplemented by two additional factors – the role of government and chance. It is noteworthy that Porter had relegated the role of government to a secondary factor as it betrays a deep ideological aversion to the role that the state might play, which is evident in all his work, especially his counter-factual account of Japanese success, *Can Japan Compete?* (Porter et al., 2000). In Porter's accounts of strategy, the state is often placed on the periphery, neatly reflecting the 'small government' sentiments of the time in which his ideas became fashionable – the period of Reaganomics and Thatcherism. Of course, such thinking has now become 'the received wisdom' but, as we shall see, it ignores certain realities. But first, what is the role of government in Porter's model?

Governments influence all four of Porter's determinants through a variety of actions, such as subsidies to firms, either directly (money) or indirectly (through infrastructure), through tax regimes, through raising industry standards, and by educational policies that affect the skill level of workers. Actually, given that governments come and go with the democratic process but that the states that they govern go on despite this, it is better to speak of the role of the state rather than the role of government. According to Porter, the role of government should be limited to: encouraging companies to raise their performance, stimulating early demand for advanced products, focusing on specialist knowledge creation through funding research institutes, concentrating on creating free markets, and seeking to minimize inflation and economic certainty. Such prescriptions could be drawn straight from an International Monetary Fund manual. It is important to remember that strategy concepts – like all theories – emerge from a time and context. They are neither value-free or neutral observations but rather are ideologically bound.

Porter's free market ideological position is quite clear. It goes a long way to explaining the downplaying of the role of the state. But is this realistic? Given that state activity accounts for 40–50 per cent of gross domestic product, it surely must be an important factor in any diamond? It is really important not to neglect the role of the state. For instance, in the USA, how can one ignore the role the state plays in the massive military-industrial complex? If we look at some of the most innovative regions, such as Huntsville, Alabama, then the US Missile and Space Programs were the mother of the considerable invention that occurred, fuelled by federal funding on a grand scale, oriented initially to supporting the research of Werner von Braun, the German rocket scientist, whom the US 'captured' at the cessation of hostilities at the end of the Second World War. Around his and related expertise, with massive federal budgets, a huge military-industrial complex was developed. As we have seen, the spectre of Japan haunted Reagan, which led to Porter researching and writing his *magnum opus*. Given the importance of Japan, the lessons Porter drew were curiously one-sided. By concentrating on the internal four dimensions of the diamond, Porter side-stepped serious consideration to the role played by the state in planning and intervening in Japanese industry. This selective blindness is striking.

We disagree with Porter and regard the state as important in any attempt to understand the economic performance of a sector in a region. Stefano Harney (2007) has also picked up on this point, arguing that strategy lacks any sophisticated theory of the state, seeing it through few terms other than those of 'red-tape' and 'bureaucracy', which correspond more to certain business prejudices than to a realistic analysis of the role of the state. It is an important omission that strategy scholarship needs to redress to try to gain a more accurate understanding of how strategy works today (see Fairbrother, 2007 for an apposite example).

chance

The final aspect of the diamond is the role of chance. Chance can intervene to strengthen or unravel a diamond. A commonly cited example of chance is in relation to Japan. Following its military defeat in August 1945, Japan was occupied by the United States army. With the defeat of fascism quickly giving away to tensions between the west and the Soviet Bloc – the Cold War – which was to last for the best part of the next fifty years, Japan assumed a vital geopolitical importance. Influenced by Keynesian ideas, the Americans wanted Japan to have a vibrant economy and a functioning liberal democracy. At all costs, it was to remain in the western sphere of influence. Supplying their vast army in Japan meant a constant convoy of large merchant and military vessels going between Japan and the United States. It was decided by US military authorities in Japan that Japanese products could be shipped to America in the largely empty vessels returning home. This helped to kick-start the war-ravaged industrial capacity of Japan. This was a chance event that had serendipitous consequences for Japanese industry.

Having explained the constituent parts of the diamond, it is important to interpret it critically. Let's restate a few points. First, a sector will have its own diamond in a given region; this diamond might be stronger, weaker or more or less the same as diamonds in other regions. Porter's argument is that the stronger a region's diamond in a particular sector, the more likely the sector will be globally competitive. Of course, this will be true by definition because the statement is a tautology. More globally competitive regions *will* be stronger than less competitive sectors. Amidst the tautologies, the message was clear: the homebase matters.

innovative capacity

When the factors are aligned, then a nation has an enhanced national innovative capacity. National innovative capacity is the potential of a country – as both a political and economic entity – to produce and commercialize a flow of innovative technology at a given point in time. Of course, to talk of national innovative capacity is to address innovation at one remove: in so far as states have an innovative capacity, it is because firms located within their boundaries do innovation. What states can do is to help enable innovation through the provision of infrastructure, such as broadband, mass, sophisticated and state-provided education, ports, railways and public transport, for instance. As such, national innovative capacity is not only deeply institutionally embedded in the work that the state has done historically, but it also depends on an ongoing and interrelated set of fundamental investments, policies and resource commitments that determine the extent and success of innovative effort in a country over the long term.

The concept of innovative capacity was first formulated in 1990 by a geographer, Luis Suarez-Villa. Similar ideas have been used in many subsequent publications by Porter and associated authors. In the work of Porter and his collaborators, national innovative capacity is seen to result from:

1 a common pool of institutions, resource commitments and policies that support innovation, referred to as the common innovation infrastructure;
2 the particular innovation orientation of groups of interconnected national industrial clusters; and
3 the quality of linkages between the two.

The common innovation system is seen in terms of a country's accumulated stock of knowledge and the extent of available scientific and technical talent dedicated to the production of new technologies. In addition, it will also depend on national investments and policy choices, such as spending on higher education, intellectual property protection, and openness to international competition, which will exert a cross-cutting impact on innovativeness across economic sectors. Influenced by this thinking, many governments around the world have developed national innovation policies designed to try to foster national innovation capacity. A major mechanism for this is often seen to be the development of industrial clusters.

The idea of clusters is an old one that goes back at least to the nineteenth-century British economist Alfred Marshall, who wrote about industrial districts in which a cluster of related competencies allows an industry to flourish. It is the firms in specific industrial clusters that introduce and commercialize innovations. There are four key contextual elements in these clusters: (1) the presence of high quality and specialized inputs; (2) a context that encourages investment and intense local rivalry; (3) pressure and insight gleaned from sophisticated local demand; and (4) the presence of a cluster of related and supporting industries. These elements have a central influence on the rate of innovation in a given national industrial cluster. Thus, national industry policy should be oriented to supporting or seeding such clusters. Where these are well developed, then there will be high-quality linkages between the four contextual factors and the innovation system, such as where local education institutions seed many local industry-related innovative firms. In the absence of a viable infrastructure of venture capital, specialized and competing local firms – that is, in the absence of the contextual elements being well-developed – then the national innovation system may remain underdeveloped even where national investments are made in the educational infrastructure.

In empirical applications of these ideas, Suarez-Villa's (1990) path-breaking work on innovation as indicated by patents is used. The findings strongly suggest that investment in higher education, the development of intellectual property rights and the existence of an economically liberal economy are essential factors in developing a successful innovative capacity strategy. However, as both Suarez-Villa's (1990) original work and Stern, Porter and Furnham's (1999) work suggests, it is educational infrastructure that is found to have the most important association with innovative capacity. Hence, the widely observed switch to systems of mass higher education in many OECD countries during the 1990s, eclipsing previously rather small and elite based systems.

would Henry Ford have succeeded had he started out in the English West Midlands?

One of our favourite strategists is Peter Clark of the University of London. His work engages very closely with Porter's diamond. In his classic book *Organisations in Action* (2000), Clark poses the counterfactual question: what would have happened had Henry Ford started out in the English industrial West Midlands? In the analytical parlour game that follows, he argues that Henry Ford would have failed because of the lack of a strong diamond for mass production in the English West Midlands. There was a constellation of poor factor conditions, especially around British understandings of scientific management, undemanding home consumers, a lack of competition (in part through protected access to British Empire markets), and rudimentary related and supporting industries. His argument runs counter to some of the more entrepreneurial explanations which would highlight the innate genius of someone like Henry Ford. Clark's analysis is a neat illustration of applying Porter's work.

The essence of Porter is that the homebase matters. Clark would agree. The policy implication for a company is to try to locate itself in a highly competitive diamond, so if you wanted to become world class in whisky production, you would probably head for Scotland rather than Japan, for instance. Porter's ideas are interesting and fun to think with. But there are of course criticisms. Porter's analysis, while claiming to be neutral, is highly ideological in presuming the supremacy of free markets and small government. It is also pretty naïve in that most large corporations operate in anything but free markets. The studies seem to fit the diamond all too neatly. It falls silent on issues of managerial and worker agency. It is supremely tautological.

conclusion

In this chapter we have introduced some of the key concepts associated with strategic management. In other words, it is the strategic management orthodoxy. Many of these ideas have been translated from industrial economics. Undoubtedly, some of the analysis works. Different industries are structured in different ways; organizations do make decisions about where to position themselves; there is a process through which goods or services are produced and some regions seem to be better at producing some goods and services than others. Porter's work gives us a way of thinking about some of these ideas. Perhaps more disturbing is the way in which Porter's ideas have travelled into organizations and governments. Rather than being *a* way of thinking about strategy, they have increasingly taken on the status of being *the* way of doing strategy. The result has been to create a self-fulfilling prophecy and tautology unencumbered by exception or doubt. Think about your region. Does the local government have a policy for creating a 'world-class' cluster? If it does, then you can probably trace that policy right back to Porter.

acknowledgements

Figures 3.1 and 3.2: Reprinted with the permission of The Free Press, a Division of Simon & Schuster Adult Publishing Group, from *Competitive Advantge: Creating and Sustanining Superior Performance* by Michael E. Porter. Copyright © 1985, 1998 by Michael E. Porter. All rights reserved.

Figure 3.3 from M. Porter, *The Competitive Advantage of Nations*, 1998, Simon & Schuster reproduced with permission of Palgrave Macmillan.

4

Strategy = Understanding What's Inside the Firm

███████ the resource-based view of strategy

We have seen that Porter's economic strategy approach focuses very much on the external environment of a firm and uses that to determine the strategy for an organization to adopt. The influence of Porter's ideas is such that they often form the intellectual backdrop for the development of regional and national strategies. The approach emphasizes responding to the external environment. Porter's ideas have taken the status of what heterodox economist Deirdre McCloskey (1985) terms 'the gnomic present' – a present tense where time and place are irrelevant because the laws of economics are always universal! One advantage of Porter's approach is that it plays directly to levers of national investment and priorities that governments control. However, it shifts discussions of strategy to an elevated level. The strategy of a firm is now seen as a lower-level contingency to the strategy of the nation. In fact, what actually occurs at the firm level slips out of the frame.

Framing an organization's strategy according to the structure of its market also poses other difficulties because it assumes that the market is relatively static or fixed in its dimensions. While this might be the case in some sectors, commentators on globalization frequently remind us that markets are changing at a rapid pace. With that in mind, what is the logic of defining an organization's strategy in relation to a market that might change very quickly? One school of thought has criticized this perspective and argued that it is the internal resources and unique capabilities that should and do drive the strategy of a firm, irrespective of more macro-level phenomena. The perspective is called the resource-based view (RBV) of the firm and has had a significant impact on strategic thinking. The resource-based view of strategy emerged as a counterpoint to Porter's and other market-based approaches, perspectives that often made heroic and fanciful assumptions. At its simplest, the resource-based view is interested in what an organization can do: it asks what are its capabilities? The RBV has become one of the most influential approaches within strategic management and, while it is different from Porter style analyses, it remains broadly mainstream and conservative in its assumptions and modelling.

The RBV's key argument is that it is internal characteristics that determine success or failure, and that firms should build their strategies on their internal strengths. According to this view, industry characteristics become less dominant and what the state or national government may or may not do is discounted. The resource-based perspective highlights the need for a fit between the external market context in which a firm operates and its internal capabilities. Smart, strategically-driven firms will seek to build these into an irreplaceable array of competencies. Instead of focusing on external conditions and constraints in the environment, the RBV suggests that strategy should provide the basis for leveraging the firm's core competencies relative to opportunities in the external environment. Accordingly, strategy focuses on the firm's unique resource positions; it is these, it argues, which produce superior products of superior performance.

▬▬▬ strategy is driven by what you are able to do and have

The intellectual origins of RBV developed from the influential economics perspective of Edith Penrose (1959). Concentrating on the resources and capabilities controlled by a firm, the RBV seeks to see how they can be used to develop strategy. Penrose sees the distinctiveness of a firm as determined by the heterogeneity of the products and services that are available or potentially available from its resources. The conditions that constrain resource heterogeneity are market imperfections and the persistence of differential 'rents' – surplus earnings over and above the norm in the industry due to some not easily imitated aspects of what and how the organization does what it can do – across firms or organizations. Market imperfections include things such as sunk costs, supply scarcities, transaction and agency costs, barriers to mobility, inadequate information, permanent commitments, and diverse access to strategic factor markets.

Edith Penrose's ideas, while influential at the time of their publication, waned in influence until they were re-animated by the work of American strategists, such as Wernerfelt (1984), who laid the foundation for the modern-day adoption of the RBV. The big idea is that organizations can be viewed as a bundle of resources, which can help them attain competitive advantage.

Wernerfelt saw resources as the key for organizational profitability. These resources can be acquired through takeovers, thus adding new resources to existing ones. Of course, resources can be exploited and developed over time as well. Hence, according to the RBV, it is not unique products (as suggested in the Boston Consulting Group matrix, for instance) but unique resources and skills that ensure organizational competitive advantage and long-term survival. For Wernerfelt, resources incorporated a diverse set of things, including knowledge, technology, skilled staff, machinery, brand names, efficient processes, etc. Other researchers have added culture and innovation capability to the mix (see Heracleous, 2003). Put simply, resources are the sum of all intangible and tangible assets that may allow an organization to develop a competitive advantage. Tangible assets such as physical plant, financial muscle or intellectual property rights are important and relatively self-explanatory; intangibles such as reputation, brands, creativity and the ability to innovate are altogether more mysterious – the so-called blackbox of the firm.

Wernerfelt's ideas were developed in the 1980s (Barney, 1986; Dierickx and Cool, 1989) and assumed a major position in strategy approaches in the 1990s. Strategists such as Barney (1991) and Grant (1991), as well as popular management writers such as Hamel and Prahalad (1990), did much to propel the perspective to the attention of academics, managers and students. For adherents of the resource-based view, competitive advantage is determined by algebraically plotting an organization's resources.

Against the industry school of Porter, the resource-based view of the firm suggests that it is not *industry* but *firm* factors that are vital. The RBV approach recognizes that organizations are different and it seeks to analyze how they differ. To do this, it posits that resources come in four types:

- financial (such as equity capital and loans)
- physical (plant, equipment and land)
- human (the experience, knowledge and training of employees)
- organizational (trust, which is sometimes referred to as embeddedness).

Two basic assumptions are implicit in the resource-based view of the firm: that resources and capabilities can vary significantly across firms (the assumption of firm heterogeneity) in a stable way (the assumption of resource immobility). The specificity of the distribution of these resources can become unique sources of competitive advantage.

what's a valuable resource?

Resources are inputs into a firm's production process and include financial capital, equipment and human capital. They are either tangible or intangible in nature. Valuable resources are those things that firms control that enable them to conceive and implement strategies to improve their efficiency and effectiveness. To count as a resource, it must be something that is rare or unique to the firm (i.e. if they are available to all firms, then they are unlikely to be a source of competitive advantage). When resources are the basis for competitive advantage, they must display four characteristics that are often referred to as the VRIN model:

1 Valuable in enabling the firm to exploit opportunities and counter threats.
2 Rare among competitor organizations.
3 Imperfectly imitable.
4 Not easily substitutable.

The VRIN model gives a good indication of how resource-base theorists think competitive advantage is derived. The RBV seeks to identify those things that organizations have that cannot easily be the basis for copying because it would be too costly to do so or competitors cannot access them. Rather than scanning the market for opportunities, strategists should be looking inside the firm to discover sources of competitive advantage. The resources that confer advantage might rise for any number of reasons. They can arise from supply scarcities based on superior resources that serve as the source of competitive advantage because they are fixed and cannot be expanded freely or imitated by other organizations. For instance, many students interested in golf choose to attend the University of St Andrews – where all of the authors have worked – because of the town's association with the home of golf. Thus, golf is a source of competitive advantage for the university, relating to the fact that there is only one home of golf.

Sometimes the reason why an organization enjoys its unique advantage is difficult to unravel from the casual mix of possible factors – there is a causal ambiguity that can, in its ineffability, become a strategic factor. The sources of advantage may be complex and somewhat intangible, such as an 'excellent' culture in Peters and Waterman's (1982) terms. For instance, St Andrews University regularly features in the list of Britain's top ten universities and so this denotes a certain intangible 'excellence'. We might think of this as a type of monopoly rent that results from market power.

Whether it is proximity to sacred sites of sport, such as the Links course at St Andrews, or excellence, as denoted by top ten lists, each of these factors bestows a specific unique capability. Most usually, these capabilities are something that is internal to the firm or organization's portfolio of activities, usually defined as a capacity for a set of resources to perform an activity. The organization develops unique expertise in using these resources, and thus its capabilities become difficult for competitors to imitate.

Managing these capabilities means having to steer a tight course between keeping things simple and routine enough to be easily managed but not so simple and routine that they are highly imitable or allowing them to become so complex that they become difficult to steer and control. Competitive advantage arises when an organization does something unique that creates value. Once it is copied then the uniqueness is gone and dynamic capability is lost. Capabilities are necessarily dynamic because they are always subject to imitation and outflanking by competitors. Competitive advantage comes from assembling and exploiting unique combinations of resources.

Sustainable competitive advantage can only be won by continuously developing existing resources incrementally while trying also to innovate products and services discontinuously in ways that play to the unique capabilities the organization has assembled, or can assemble, as it responds to changing market conditions.

The RBV has been subject to considerable criticism. Priem and Butler (2001), for example, argue that the RBV is tautological because we cannot know whether a firm has unique capabilities independently of the description of them. Hence their description cannot function as an explanation. Additionally, it could be that many different configurations of resource could generate similar value for firms and, thus, it would be incorrect to see just one of these as the source of competitive advantage. It also presumes that a neat causality can be drawn between a resource and competitive advantage – the links might be far from uni-directional or clear. The extent to which the RBV, with its internal focus, really addresses markets on which products and services compete is not clear. Organizations may have unique capabilities that produce unique products and services and still fail on the market because of external factors that they cannot control, such as the emergence of international standards that are inimical to their positioning. Also, similarly to Porter, the implications for actual organizations are unclear: what should firms' strategists actually do to build unique capabilities if they do not currently have them?

Other criticisms of the RBV suggest that it is difficult to find resources that satisfy the VRIN criteria. Most internal resources can be copied and even the highly idiosyncratic skills of leading researchers, for instance, can be poached by competitor institutions. A further criticism concerns the role of intangible resources in creating competitive advantages. Patents, proprietary technologies or relationships may explain performance heterogeneity among firms and be the likely sources of competitive advantage, but it is the bundle of resources and the quality of their relationships overall that may be vital. Having VRIN resources which relate badly to more orthodox elements of the organization is not in the organization's best interests. Moreover, external, environmental factors, such as those proposed in Michael Porter's industry structure analysis, should also be considered.

Finally, the sustainability of maintaining inimitable resources over the long term must be questioned: patents can be unravelled and can be copied, backwards engineering can replicate the outcomes of inimitable resources, and star talent can be attracted to competitors. The dynamism of the inimitable capabilities may be too high for prolonged strategic success.

RBV has aroused considerable excitement in strategy. In pursuing this line of thought strategists come up against the limitations of their own discipline. They make a convincing case that there is something going on in the firm that is mysterious, fluid, and improvisational that, in some ways, links to competitive advantage. They have discovered a blackbox, wherein the intriguing secrets of competitive advantage lie, but the problem is that the conservative doctrine of mainstream strategy does little to help them access such knowledge. The RBV is handicapped by the economic assumptions that frame its analysis. Within the frame of economic rationalism the source of competitive advantage becomes the irrational, the ineffable, the something or other that makes a company go from good to great. Strategy analysis becomes akin to the search for the Holy Grail.

beyond the search for the Holy Grail?

In its emphasis on the particular and inimitable, the RBV represents the flip-side of institutional theory. Institutional theory suggests that, for cultural reasons, some designs and practices become regarded, for whatever reasons, as highly esteemed, as displaying high 'cultural capital'. Through one or more of three specific mechanisms (coercive, mimetic or normative isomorphism), specific strategic templates becomes widely adopted and become the standard way of operating. Thus, there are a limited number of explanations as to why so many organizations around the world adopted the bureaucratic form or the multi-divisional structure. One explanation would stress biological necessity: it might be genetic to create and order life according to hierarchies, and thus unavoidable – something imprinted in the species' way of doing things. Another explanation would stress efficiency: bureaucracy is functional, simply the one best way to organize large-scale activities under uncertain conditions. Finally, another explanation is that bureaucracy has become so conventional that we find it normal to mimic the bureaucratic form because it has become so widely institutionalized. The reasons for its institutionalization (that it was associated with actions widely admired) have faded with time, such that it now seems natural, normal and necessary. The last argument is now widely accepted and is known as institutional theory. Institutional theory was developed in the 1950s and 1960s and early contributions emphasized the role of conflict and of the negotiated order between different interest groups. More recently, new institutional theory emerged and shifted the emphasis towards understanding how organizations appear legitimate in the eyes of stakeholders.

Institutional theory has been particularly influential in organization studies. Organization studies, drawing on social anthropology and industrial sociology, offers understanding of what goes on inside a firm and seeks to uncover the rationalities-in-use by the actors rather than merely supplementing the rationalities-in-use by economists. However, the adaptation of sociology and anthropology to management's remit has, unfortunately, not put paid to fruitless searches for a Holy Grail – but it has changed its nature. If the Holy Grail of the economists is the pearl that grows around the grit of difference inside the rational shell of the firm, then for those who have channelled anthropology and sociology, the search is less for a difference that is hard to grasp but more for the tacit knowledge of those who comprise the firm, which, it will turn out, is even harder to grasp. Even those who have it don't know they have it and don't even know what 'it' is! Recent developments in management have sought to understand the structuring of knowledge within the firm and this has developed into a sub-discipline known as Knowledge Management. Put simply, Knowledge Management seeks to understand the way in which organizations create new knowledge and exploit knowledge within the firm. Much of the literature on Knowledge Management lays emphasis on how organizations go about 'capturing' knowledge from the mind of the worker and placing it under the proprietorial ownership of the firm, re-badging Taylorism for the twenty-first century as an appropriation of the ineffable within each of us.

Perhaps aware of the banality of their pedigree, many Knowledge Management scholars shroud themselves in philosophical mysticism and seem never happier than when referring back to ancient Greek nostrums about knowledge. With a few notable exceptions, Knowledge Management has constructed a series of endlessly self-referential discussions that tell us little about the structuring of knowledge in and around organizations. Rather than the ancient Greeks, a look at *Through the Looking Glass*, or even *Dracula*, might prove a better starting point.

Knowledge Management

According to the RBV, it is what a firm knows that it has which is different that is really strategically important. According to aficionados of Knowledge Management (KM), it is what a firm doesn't know that it has which it can convert to what it does know that is different, which is really strategically important: tacit knowledge.

In Lewis Carroll's *Through the Looking Glass*, the White Queen tells Alice that to believe in the impossible is merely a matter of drawing a deep breath and shutting her eyes: 'Why, sometimes I've believed as many as six impossible things before breakfast', the White Queen admonished (Carroll, 1982: 173). While the influence of Nonaka and Takeuchi's (1995) work has seen the institutionalization of Michael Polanyi's distinction between 'tacit knowledge' and 'explicit knowledge', it has led to the concept of tacit knowledge being misunderstood (Tsoukas, 2003).

Polanyi's (1967) observation that '*we can know more than we can tell*' is cited by Nonaka and Takeuchi as part of their claim that, given appropriate effort, cognitive tacit knowledge can be articulated: 'the articulation of tacit mental models, in a kind of "mobilization" process, is a key factor in creating new knowledge' (Nonaka and Takeuchi, 1995: 60). And western managers have seized on the idea that tacit knowledge is a hidden resource than can be commodified and managed. Part of KM's allure seems to stem from the idea that it would make 'what knowledge workers know' explicit and 'empower' managers.

Tacit–explicit knowledge conversion appears to be a way of converting the personal capacity 'to know' (tacit knowledge) into an object (explicit knowledge) that can be *managed*. Explicit knowledge is presented as a universally comprehensible commodity, which can be stored in a knowledge archive, shared with colleagues or clicked across cyberspace. The core of KM centres on tacit–explicit knowledge conversion. In an incisive essay entitled 'Do we really understand tacit knowledge?', Haridimos Tsoukas (2003) makes the crucial point that Nonaka and Takeuchi's book, *The Knowledge-Creating Company* (1995), has helped to institutionalize an erroneous view of Polanyi's insight into tacit knowing. Short of a brain transplant, the capacity to know is not a transferable commodity: it is inherently personal and inherently tacit: '*All knowledge falls into one of these two classes: it is either tacit or rooted in tacit knowledge*' (Polanyi, 1967: 195, original emphasis). An individual's active shaping of his or her experience can become the subject of conscious thought through the Gestalt integration of unspecified particulars that lie outside consciousness. But, contrary to Nonaka and Takeuchi's argument, Polanyi's use of Gestalt psychology made it logically impossible to be explicit about the particulars of a tacit integration: 'We can only point to the existence of tacit integration in our experience. We must be forever unable to give it an explicit specification' (Polanyi and Prosch, 1975: 62).

> The ideal of a strictly explicit knowledge is indeed self-contradictory; deprived of their tacit coefficients, all spoken words, all formulae, all maps and graphs, are strictly meaningless. An exact mathematical theory means nothing unless we recognize an inexact non-mathematical knowledge on which it bears and a person whose judgment upholds this bearing. (Polanyi, 1967: 195)

But, in a manner that might make the White Queen proud, 'strictly meaningless' explicit knowledge is presented – in Polanyi's name – as the mainspring of Nonaka and Takeuchi's (1995) argument. KM appears to be a bewitchment of our intelligence by the language of explicit knowledge. Early evidence suggested that KM could offer an opportunity to 'learn from failure' (Storey and Barnett, 2000). In *The Knowledge-Creating Company: How Japanese Companies Create the*

Dynamics of Innovation (Nonaka and Takeuchi, 1995: 11), which has become a hugely influential 'lesson from Japan', the central message is simple: 'The explanation of how Japanese companies create new knowledge boils down to the conversion of tacit knowledge to explicit knowledge'.

> Tacit knowledge is highly personal and hard to formalize, making it difficult to communicate or to share with others. Subjective insights, intuitions, and hunches fall into this category of knowledge. ... To be more precise, tacit knowledge can be segmented into two dimensions. The first is the technical dimension, which encompasses the kind of informal and hard-to-pin-down skills or crafts captured in the term 'know-how'. ... At the same time, tacit knowledge contains an important cognitive dimension. It consists of schemata, mental models, beliefs, and perceptions so ingrained that we take them for granted. The cognitive dimension of tacit knowledge reflects our image of reality (what is) and our vision for the future (what ought to be). (Nonaka and Takeuchi, 1995: 8)

Whereas:

> Explicit knowledge can be expressed in words and numbers, and easily communicated and shared in the form of hard data, scientific formulae, codified procedures, or universal principles. Thus knowledge is viewed synonymously with a computer code, a chemical formula, or a set of general rules. (Nonaka and Takeuchi, 1995: 8)

And:

> For tacit knowledge to be communicated and shared within the organization, it has to be converted into words or numbers that anyone can understand. It is precisely during this time that conversion takes place – from tacit to explicit, and, as we shall see, back again into tacit – that organizational knowledge is created. (Nonaka and Takeuchi, 1995: 9)

Allegedly, tacit–explicit knowledge conversion enables 'inexpressible language' associated with an individual's 'cognitive tacit knowledge' to be expressed as explicit knowledge, which is presented as a universally comprehensible language: it comprises words or numbers that can be understood by 'anyone'. Astonishingly, many in the strategic manage-ment community seem happy to take the concept of translation from implicit, tacit, personal knowledge to explicit knowledge seriously. But, just think what is being proposed: subjective sensemaking can be con-verted into an object among other objects. Such objects might include 'scientific formulae' and 'universal principles' that western traditions normally associate with objective knowledge. Hence, objectivity can be synthesized from subjectivity. For Nonaka and Takeuchi, *amplifying* and *crystallizing* the knowledge of an individual produces universally applicable explicit knowledge. As has been argued at length elsewhere, the process assumes a set of standing conditions that may, for specific institutional reasons, be found in some Japanese companies but are not necessarily to be found elsewhere (Ray and Clegg, 2007).

Peter Drucker called Nonaka and Takeuchi's (1995) book a 'clas-sic' (Takeuchi and Nonaka, 2004: ix). During the late 1990s, refer-ences to KM mushroomed. The editors of a major handbook on organizational learning and knowledge management suggest that Nonaka and Takeuchi (1995) 'set the standard' for the emergent field of 'organizational knowledge' (Easterby-Smith and Lyles, 2003: 11), while the editors of *Organization*'s January 2007 special issue on 'The Philosophical Foundations of Knowledge Management' sug-gested that Nonaka and Takeuchi's book is 'surely KM's most influen-tial work' (Spender and Scherer, 2007: 5). If that is the case, then the quality of KM's contribution to strategy is minimal. As remarked ear-lier, it promises, at best, an Alice in Wonderland; at worst, it proposes what elsewhere has been called an 'organizational gothic' (Garrick and Clegg, 2000) at the heart of organizational life: a capacity to suck the vitality from the individual body and soul in order to enhance the vitality of the corporate body for increased efficiency and reduced costs, through alchemy. Quite how and why individuals might be able, or even want to, surrender up what they only know they know tacitly, so that it can be made explicit for others, is not at all clear.

In the previous chapter, we saw the far-reaching influence that Porter's ideas have had on the organizational world. To what extent has RBV and KM made an impact on the organizational world? Knowledge Management has been something of a management fash-ion in recent years, with many organizations adopting KM initiatives as a means of leveraging and exploiting knowledge. We know from the management fashion literature that many organizations will have adopted such ideas to appear 'up-to-date' and stylish. Chief Knowledge Officers were a good look in the management fashion stakes for a few years, but could they really unlock value through the alchemy of making the tacit explicit? Nigel Thrift, in a recent article, suggests that significant changes are occurring in the formation of capitalism. He argues that primitive capitalism, such as the extraction of oil, mining, etc., is taking place with an unprecedented vigour, while simultaneously in the post-industrial western countries there is the development of 'full palette capitalism' which seeks to 'squeeze every last drop of value out of the system by increasing the rate of innovation and invention' (Thrift, 2006: 281). Full palette capitalism marks the bringing together of an assemblage of factors like RBV and Knowledge Management with changes in the financial markets. It is to finance – more particularly, private equity – that we now turn.

private equity funds

At the core of any theory of economics is the notion of capital as a bundle of property rights and relations that take material form in sets of resources – of land, labour and capital – and perhaps some ineffable intangibles. These resources become institutionalized in their relations, bound by collective agreements with employees, vested in major portfolios of financial houses and superannuation funds, as well as becoming girt by the career aspirations and achievements of the managers who service them.

While institutional theorists may see institutionalization as a largely one-way street, economists do not. If the resources that are institutionalized could be de-institutionalized, if the resources bundled up in the firm could be unbundled, wouldn't this allow an unlocking of the value within? While acquisitions and management buy-outs have long been part of stock market capitalism, the recent trend for private equity offers something new both in its scale and intensity. Stephen Ackroyd, a strategist at Lancaster University, is currently researching the private equity industry. He regards it as a movement that marks a shift in the British economy in that major companies are going through a transformation. His argument is that if you look at the London Stock Exchange, the top 15 companies, in terms of market capitalization, are worth around US$ 1 trillion, while the remaining 185 on the FTSE are worth $1.6 trillion. This bifurcation in the stock market means that the top 15 are genuinely global actors, while the remainder – worth between $1 billion and $10 billion – are vulnerable to private equity takeover. In recent years, such household names as Boots, Cadbury-Schweppes and Sainsbury's have all been targets for private equity takeover. For instance, in the UK, one of the capitals of the private equity movement, over 1.2 million employees work for private equity firms, which accounts for around 20 per cent of the British private sector workforce. Private equity firms work on the premise that they can buy stock-exchange listed firms and take them off the stock exchange and then put in more aggressive and efficient managers to run them. A private equity takeover is often quickly followed by a bout of downsizing and cost-cutting.

Much of the money made available to the private equity capitalists comes from sovereign funds. For instance, countries such as China, Singapore and Norway have huge funds available for investing in private equity schemes. Oddly enough, in view of the oft-repeated mantras of neo-liberal economists who claim that government has no business being involved in business, much of the world economy is increasingly held in state-financed entities – sometimes even buying businesses that were de-nationalized in the first place because of neo-liberal commitments! A private equity deal will generally be saturated with debt and require the organization to make high returns. The link with resource-based thinking is that the attractive firms for private equity deals are those with strong brands and an apparent competitive advantage in their sector. Private equity capitalists view organizations as a bundle of resources that can be exploited, which is akin to RBV theorists seeing the organization as a bundle of resources that create competitive advantage. In a recent report by Thornton (2007: 22) it has been argued that 'it seems evident that private equity firms have been able to extract previously hidden value in the companies they take over'.

As we have argued, the RBV is part mysticism, part tautology. When it is joined up with the power of privatized capital in private equity it becomes altogether more clandestine and open to obfuscation. The reason for this is that private equity firms do not have the same disclosure requirements as stock exchange listed firms. By being de-listed from the stock exchange, private equity firms are insulated from having to disclose earnings and profits. Many stakeholders within civil society have argued that this results in an alarming lack of corporate accountability such that it is very difficult to understand what an organization is up to, how it is funded, and its general sustainability as an ongoing proposition. Is the value being sucked out of it to service debt and yield a substantial return when it is sold on? Trade unions remain concerned that private equity leads to an intensification of work conditions, a reneging of pension agreements and an increased chance of being made redundant.

Stephen Ackroyd is very suspicious about the claims of private equity, seeing it as a pernicious and damaging, not to mention extremely secretive, form of capitalism. He contrasts this with corporate capitalism:

> We, the British state, have presided over this bargain basement sale, not putting an end to it, whilst compromising the pension entitlements of a large section of the population. So I never thought I would be making talks in favour of corporate capitalism but it seems to me to be relatively benign, if you are going to have capitalism, corporate capitalism is relatively benign because in certain ways it is open to inspection, open to criticism. … Private capitalism doesn't have these qualities. You can't get the accounts and you don't know how many people they employ. Certainly, fairly obvious indicators for researchers are unavailable. (Ackroyd, 2007)

The big winners from private equity deals seem to be the private equity capitalists, the finance houses that put together the deals and the managers who are brought in to run the firms. For some, private equity is a form of casino capitalism that poses grave risks to the economy in return for massive short-term gain for a small group of capitalists whose view of the firm is only that it is 'resource-based' and, if they own these resources privately, they can do with them what they will.

In this sense, the RBV gives private equity capitalists the rationale and language to justify their actions.

Private equity points to the importance of 'financialization' more generally. Financialization is the process through which finance capital – and its attendant logic – penetrates more and more parts of the organizational world. Some authors see the rise of financialization as a movement ushered in by the changes that took place in the 1990s, signalled by the discourses of 'economic value added' and 'value-based management' initiatives gaining ascendancy as part of the more general Shareholder Value Movement. Froud et al. point out the contradiction of financialization. As it ramps up the return on capital employed (ROCE), the performance expectations of firms escalates to the point that managers are asked to 'deliver the undeliverable' (Froud et al., 2000: 106). The ineffable has been operationally redefined as 'extraordinary returns' and what achieves it is of little consequence because the whole point of such returns is their potential for further gain by selling these resources on. Accordingly, Froud and his colleagues identify the ideology of the 'new' competition:

1   Financialization compares firms, across different sectors and places a similar performance criteria on them, which intensifies pressure on 'lower performing' industries.
2   Firms that remain listed are likely to experience far greater pressure from their shareholders over issues of corporate strategy as they are outperformed by private equity in the short term and as private equity sales yield huge surpluses in the mid-term.
3   Performance will be more narrowly conceived in financial terms.
4   There will be an intensification of managerial work as managers try to deal with the contradictions of a position that has become much more exposed to the identification of the contribution they are making to revenue, and which can only too easily be sold out from under them.

While it is important to be wary of declarations that the nature of finance has changed, only to find that a few years later it reverts to type once more, financialization and private equity firms provide a glimpse into one possible future as a harbinger of a world yet to come.

conclusion

The upshot of a resource-based view of the firms is a focus on what these resources can yield today in their present combination and what they could yield in the near future – in two or three years – under a different set of combinatorial possibilities. Knowledge Management differs little. Its view is that by making the tacit knowledge of employees explicit, then competitive advantage in the near future will flow from knowing in the future what it doesn't know its employees don't know they know now. Finally, when the search for these Holy Grails is exhausted, and there is sufficient commitment to believe that de-institutionalization can point the way to where it may be found through extraordinary returns, then the resources can be 'liberated' from the market and the blackbox of the firm become ever blacker and more impenetrable. Private equity is an epiphenomenon of how markets and competition are changing and strategy, the handmaiden of capital, is nothing if it is not dynamic. Increasingly, the world being created by business is one in which influential ideas, such as the RBV, exhibit a performative quality. By this, we mean that they do not so much reflect the world out there as actively create it (see MacKenzie, 2007). Strategy's point is not merely to represent the world that is but to be the harbinger of a world that might become.

5

Strategy is Dead. Long Live Scenario Planning!

▬▬▬ scenario planning

'The future isn't anymore what it used to be.' This statement is attributed to Yogi Berra, the famous baseball coach. On the first glance it might sound paradoxical, but looking again it neatly makes a point that keeps strategists sleepless: the unpredictability of the future. Ex-trader turned best-selling pop-philosopher Taleb describes these issues in his book *The Black Swan* (2007). He differentiates between two (imaginary) countries: Mediocristan and Extremistan. In Mediocristan, the future is (more or less) an extrapolation of the past. Surprises do happen, but they are very rare and their impact on the average development decreases with their probability. Also, the average plays an important role in forecasting the future: if I tell you that there are two people with a combined height of 3.40 metres in a room, your best guess is to assume that each of them is 1.70 metres tall. It is not very likely that one is 3 metres and the other one only 40 centimetres. In Mediocristan, strategy is a matter of computing power: the more facts of the past you include in your calculation, the more likely it will be that you can guess what the future will be like. It's a trivial world.

The point that Taleb makes is that we live in a much more complex world – in Extremistan. Here the simple laws of Mediocristan do not apply. Rather, small causes can have massive and unexpected consequences. Think of how the First World War was triggered with the assassination of an 'Archduke', Franz Ferdinand of Austria, in the context of an arms race, repressed nationalism, and a complex system of alliances, which all contributed to the hostilities that began less than two months later. Nobody anticipated how many victims and how much misery it would bring. Think of the Internet: when it was invented as a fallback communications strategy in case of nuclear catastrophe, no one could assume that it would become such a powerful and life-changing technology. Think of J.K. Rowling's Harry Potter: nobody could know that she, sitting in a cheap Edinburgh coffee shop writing novels on a government social security scheme, would become the most widely read author of our times, making the most incredible multiplier of almost any government innovation programme ever funded.

All these extremely important events can only be explained after they happened, but no one can predict them based on past data. In Extremistan, small effects can have massive consequences. Importantly, in Extremistan, the average tells you nothing about the state of affairs. We saw that it is useful to assume an average when we talk about heights of human beings. However, Taleb gives the example of two randomly picked US citizens. Let's say their combined income is US$1 million. The most likely distribution is not $500,000 each, but $50,000 and $950,000 each. The same goes for book sales: if two books sell 1,000,000 copies combined, the most likely breakdown is not 500,000 copies each, but rather 993,000 for one and only 7,000 for the other (Taleb, 2007: 235). The same goes for financial markets: they do not yield an average return over, let's say, the past fifty years; rather, the ten most extreme days over the past fifty years represent half of the returns (Taleb, 2007: 275).

Taleb (2007: 35) describes the key difference between Mediocristan and Extremistan as follows: 'Mediocristan is where we must endure the tyranny of the collective, the routine, the obvious, and the predicted; Extremistan is where we are subjected to the tyranny of the singular, the accidental, the unseen, and the unpredicted.' Using an idea from the philosopher Bertrand Russell, Taleb invites you to conduct the following thought experiment: Imagine you are a turkey. You are fed every day and treated very well by your owner. Over, let's say, a period of 1,000 days your experience is the same, day in day out. So you think it's safe to predict the future on the past events. However, on Thanksgiving Day, just after you received an extra large portion of food, the owner grabs you, wrings your neck and you end up as a roast. You have consistently learned from the past that life is good, but extrapolating from the past into the future can give you a very wrong feeling of safety and knowledge about the future. The point is that we may be in a similar situation to the turkey – stuffed for reasons that prove terminal. Taleb sees this as weaving a narrative fallacy, putting together a seamless causal explanation that ignores many other interpretations. We can read the newspaper every day and study every textbook on best management practice, but there is no reason that the past will repeat itself in the future. Rather, it is likely that an event will occur that fundamentally changes the future.

The problem is not (only) that we cannot calculate and predict what will happen next in Extremistan; the biggest problem is rather that we naïvely assume that economists and statisticians can guide us safely through this turbulent world. They cannot. The only thing they do is make us feel more comfortable and more ignorant of the fact that we have to be much more careful with our actions. In this respect, knowledge is dangerous: the more knowledge of the past we have, the more certain we are about our judgements. Think of the turkey. Every day of being fed was another confirmation that its hypothesis of a friendly world is right. Our knowledge does not help us to forecast the future, but it makes us more certain that our guesses are the right ones. In other words, it makes us opinionated and lets us believe that we know and makes us feel more confident – without making our predictions more accurate. Put simply, the more you know, the more you believe that your forecast is right, but you are not more often right than non-experts. Hence, the key function of forecasting is 'anxiety relief for bureaucrats' (Taleb, 2007: 162), not more adequate strategy-making.

One productive way of taking the properties of Extremistan seriously, and accepting the random nature of future events and developing strategies around the unknown unknowns, is scenario planning.

strategy isn't calculating but playing with futures

Scenario planning arose, indirectly, out of a war. In 1973 the Second Arab–Israeli War occurred, when the Israeli armed forces blitzkreiged across neighbouring territories to defeat the Arab forces massed against them. The Arab response was swift and potent: the Organization of Petroleum Exporting Countries (OPEC) immediately started to raise the price of crude oil through an effective cartel, which, by the later 1970s, had a substantial effect on crude oil prices. As demand collapsed in the face of the escalating prices of crude oil, the subsequent 'oil crisis' had a major impact on western oil companies. In the past, their future strategies had always been based on an extrapolation from past trends: demand was predicted to grow quite evenly with population growth, growth in auto use and GDP, and other easily extrapolatable measures. But these extrapolations assumed that the environmental conditions characterizing the past were going to be much the same in the future. There was an assumption of continuity – rather than of the radical discontinuity that the OPEC cartel produced.

All oil companies were hard hit equally, but one responded in a way that dealt effectively with the new world of strategic planning – a world where the past did not simply extrapolate into the future. That company was Royal Dutch Shell, where, under the inspired leadership of Pierre Wack, the Shell approach of scenario planning was born. Essentially, this consisted of trying to envisage what the best- and worst-case scenarios for the future might be, and what sorts of factors might be critical in dealing with them. In practical terms, the scenarios could be constructed from strategic conversations held with the senior executive team of the organization, using some simple questions as the trigger. Armed with a range of scenarios, and a range of strategic responses to deal with them, organizations could be more fleet-footed and nimble in responding to their environments than if they just assumed that the future was an extrapolation from the past. Books such as Ringland's (1998, 2002) helped these ideas become widely adopted.

scanning the environment

Scenario planners begin by enquiring into four environmental factors that they see as framing an organization's future.

1 *Social dynamics*, including quantitative, demographic issues (e.g. increased immigration and visible minorities, the ageing of the baby boomers and next-generation successors to Generation-Xers) and softer issues of values, lifestyle, demand or political energy (the way that the 'War on Terror' seems to entail more surveillance and less autonomy).

2 *Economic issues*, including macroeconomic trends and forces shaping the economy as a whole, microeconomics (e.g. competition between small, innovator companies) and unique resource-based internal forces (e.g. employee training).

3 *Technological issues*, including direct (e.g. updating and innovating technologies or software), enabling (e.g. autonomous banking) and indirect (e.g. increased need for security experts) issues.

4 *Political issues*, including regulatory issues, such as the likely framing of future policies as more or less neo-economically liberal in key areas such as health, education and transport.

Essentially, scenario planners seek to build up a composite answer to a series of questions, answers to which will frame the imaginable boundaries for future action.

⬛ ...and more questions...

The actual questions that scenario planners will use vary, creatively, from case to case as they explore each case's specificities. Typically, however, they seek insight into the following areas.

Themes	Questions	Rationale
The vital issues	*Would you identify what you see as the critical issues for the future? When the conversation slows, continue with the comment: Suppose, I had full foreknowledge of the outcome as a genuine clairvoyant, what else would you wish to know? (Strategic drivers)*	Here the scenario planner is searching for data on where an industry or organization is going; and what events might influence it events that are forcing the organization to change.
A favourable outcome	*If things were to turn out really well for the organization, being optimistic but realistic, talk about what you see as a desirable outcome. (Questions that really matter: positive scenario factors)*	Here the scenario planner is searching for data on what really might make the organization successful.

Themes	Questions	Rationale
An unfavourable outcome	*If things went really badly, what would be the key factors that you would need to manage to try to prevent this happening? (Questions that really matter: negative scenario factors)*	Here the scenario planner seeks out information on what threatens the organization, what is putting it at risk?
Internal systems	*Where culture, structure or processes will need to change: What do you think the organization would have to do to achieve the desired future? (Preferable actions)*	With these questions the scenario planner is trying to find out what the organization members know about what it will have to do.
Lessons from past successes and failures	*Looking back, what would you identify as the significant events that have produced the current situation? (Critical Pathways)*	Here the analyst is seeking to identify what have been the key drivers for the construction of the present reality.
Decisions that have to be faced	*Looking forward, what would you see as the priority actions that should be carried out soon? (Strategic priorities)*	With this question the scenario planner seeks to isolate those factors necessary for the change scenario to be implemented.
If you were responsible	*If all constraints were removed and you could direct what is done, what more would you wish to include? (The 'Epitaph' question)*	Here the scenario planner thinks beyond the constraints of business as usual and explores the future.

These questions, which were developed initially in Shell by Gareth Price, of the St Andrews' Management Institute (SAMI), and recorded in print in Ringland (1998: 87–8), are used to frame a series of interviews with the top management team and any other members of the organization thought appropriate.

crafting answers

All the data will be recorded so that the scenario planners can work on it. In this process the data becomes a mirror on the organization and its themes rather than something owned by particular individuals. The data becomes the focus for discussion with the management team at a subsequent meeting. Working with the members at that meeting, the scenario planners will identify critical uncertainties and what members think should be done about them.

The key factors then form the basis for different scenarios. These scenarios describe how the driving forces might plausibly behave, based on the assumption of the predetermined elements and critical uncertainties. For example, in the recording industry, three scenarios may be created, depending on the degree of proliferation of websites like Kaaza. In scenario 1, a large number of music lovers spend their time downloading music and get out of the habit of buying CDs. Scenario 2 is the opposite: people become more oriented to buying CDs because downloading does not offer any added value or absolutely superb reproduction. But there is also a third possible scenario – faster growth for the recording industry because more people spend their time with a variety of music, including on the Internet, which mutually reinforce the demand for each type of consumable. Driving forces, predetermined elements and critical uncertainties structure the exploration of the future.

To create the scenario stories the planner leads the members of the organization to determine which of the driving forces are most important, what is most uncertain and what seems inevitable? The idea is to develop narratives that best capture the dynamics of the situation. Once the scenarios have been developed in some detail – usually about three – then it is time to identify what decisions need to be made. If a decision works only for one of several scenarios, then it is risky. The question that should be discussed by management is how the strategy should be adapted to make it more robust if the desired scenario doesn't plan out as predicted. As soon as the different scenarios have been defined, then a few indicators should be selected with which to monitor emergent strategy. If the scenarios have been carefully developed, they will identify and translate movements on some key indicators into an orderly set of implications, rather like a game of chess where the opponents are constantly seeking to outmanoeuvre the other player's potential moves – just as their opponents are doing to them.

The most important difference between rational approaches to strategic planning and scenario planning is the idea that the past does not progress linearly into the future. Rather, as the example of the oil crisis indicates, environments develop surprisingly quickly and dynamically. A purely rational and analytical planning process is thus an inadequate means of managing strategically. Scenario planning, on the other hand, points towards a more complex and more refined way of developing strategies: challenging taken-for-granted assumptions and questioning the status quo provides an organization with the flexibility it needs to master turbulent environments.

While scenario planning may well have the capacity to allow strategists to think creatively about their organization's future, there are dangers with the technique. The politics of the organization may make it impossible to contemplate particular futures – some statements may be inadmissible or even unthinkable. Who is participating in the scenario-making programme is also significant. For whatever the espoused plans, it more often than not ends up being the preserve of powerful, white, middle-class men giving their opinions, that is, powerful voices prevail at the expense of the weak, young or marginalized. Turning the interview responses into a set of 'robust' scenarios involves the scenario planners analyzing data and writing up different futures. The act of editing works up three 'plausible' scenarios that inevitably bear the imprint of the scenario planner as someone aiming to look good in the eyes of the client. Only certain things will be admissible in this process.

Scenario planners make much of the difference between themselves and economic forecasters and, undoubtedly, scenarios constitute a more creative means of making strategy. Scenario planners do not extrapolate data from the past but do, very often, extrapolate past assumptions, expectations and mindsets, even as they try to craft scenarios that challenge these assumptions. Scenario projects often exhibit the rationality and, dare we say it, procedural bureaucracy, of forecasting, which, rhetorically, they treat with disdain. Of course, scenario planning is but one means of trying to produce rationality about the future, albeit one which is more creative and interesting than forecasting. A case could be made that it is a critical resource for strategists, while others might cast it as a frivolous parlour game. Of course, it might be both. We are not sure what it can tell us about the future, but it can give us a fascinating glimpse into the key issues that preoccupy the powerful people of today.

future perfect strategy

Scenarios are constructed by scenario planners. However, research into a complex project by Pitsis et al. (2003) suggests that the everyday actors themselves can use some of its techniques to be their own strategists. Tyrone Pitsis and his colleagues studied a major construction project built in the run-up to the millennial Olympics held in Sydney. The project was a 20km tunnel under North Sydney, which sought to deal with the problem of severe storms overloading the waste-water system, backing up into the sewer lines and depositing the overflow into the clear blue waters of the harbour, turning them a dirty and smelly brown where the effluent entered the harbour. As with all large sporting occasions (the Olympics, football or rugby World Cups, etc.), there are vast investments made in the infrastructure of the host city. Large construction projects are notorious for running over time, over budget and lapsing into internecine legal warfare as different parties seek to blame each other for the resulting project failure. The construction project that Pitsis et al. studied had an express commitment to doing things differently and breaking the old acrimonious mindset. They sought to achieve in less than half the time a superior result to that which would have been achieved if they had adopted what the project managers termed the BAU (business as usual) approach.

Pitsis et al.'s research chronicled the implementation of a future perfect strategy, which sought to break down the BAU mentality and achieve exemplary results. So what did they mean by the future perfect? This concept has its intellectual origins in Alfred Schutz's classic work from the 1970s, which was subsequently incorporated into management studies by Karl Weick (1979, 1995). The future perfect strategy uses the imagination to picture future actions as if they had already taken place. So, in the case of the project Pitsis et al. studied, it meant imagining that the 20km tunnel traversing through subterranean North Sydney was already built. By treating the event as having already taken place, actors could then reflect on what they would have to do to achieve what they had visualized in order to realize the goal of an on-time, on-budget, socially responsible construction process. The social responsibility angle was seeded in the strategic approach of the alliance that built the tunnel. They established five key performance indicators (KPIs) for the project. These were cost, schedule, ecology, community and occupational health and safety. They then established a 'risk/reward' scheme whereby if *all* the KPIs were met, bonuses would be shared between all actors in the project, including the workforce and sub-contractors. However, if they failed to meet *all* KPIs, penalties would be similarly shared. The five KPIs were designed to be non-negotiable: it was not possible to do really well on some of them and not so well on others and still gain the bonus – this was only available if all KPIs were met or exceeded. The project used future perfect strategies to achieve exemplary outcomes.

There were three ways in which the project managers, engineers and teams associated with the tunnel project achieved the future perfect strategy. The first was through 'strange conversations', whereby a process of asking awkward, contrary and left-field questions elicited responses that added to the project manager's sense of the previously unstated assumptions and problems associated with the project. Strange conversations are a methodological practice that is commonly associated with Garfinkel – the famous 1960s American ethnomethodologist. The second method used to realize the future perfect strategy was the process of 'endgaming' through workshops. This entailed projecting into the future about when deadlines should be achieved and then working back to the present in order to come up with concrete action plans that could achieve the deadlines in the available time. The third method involved 'projecting feelings', where a great deal of time was put into understanding how people felt about aspects of the project – both within the project team and in the community more generally. The emphasis was on social empathy, which marked a radical departure from the more typically macho and laconic world that is the construction site.

What Pitsis et al.'s research findings offer strategy is an interesting means of thinking about the future and the development of strategy. The future perfect is a concept which has yet to be taken up by strategists, but it offers rich insights in terms of how to strategize for the future and the means through which this can take place – strange conversations, endgaming and projecting feelings. It could well be a useful means of challenging the BAU mentality that is so prevalent in strategy-making.

Risk Society

In democracies, elections are essentially exercises in scenario planning and party policy manifestos and launches demonstrate which risks a party – as an organization developing its strategy for election – thinks are the significant ones. The authors of this book live in Australia and the UK, respectively. In both of these jurisdictions, electioneering has become an art form, one that owes far more to strategy and Machiavelli than any manual on psephology. If a party gets its strategy wrong – and parties do, spectacularly sometimes – then its chances of re-election are at risk. It is hardly any easier for commercial organizations to manage risk than it is for political parties, especially in a world in which risk is escalating and increasingly uncontrollable – the scenario of Ulrich Beck's (2002) *Risk Society*. We will look at the 'Risk Society' thesis because, if Beck is correct, it has major implications for strategy.

Ulrich Beck's 'Risk Society' thesis is one of the more influential sociological theories to be developed over the last twenty years. Beck argues that modernity, as characterized by big science and technological programmes, and for our purposes strategic planning, has given away to a second age of modernity or 'reflexive modernization'. This era is defined, in part, by the institutions of modernity creating the very problems they sought to solve. Beck (2006) argues that risk is an omnipresent feature of society, hence the label 'Risk Society'. Beck defines the Risk Society as one in which the processes of modernization have introduced systemic risks and insecurities previously unknown in nature (Beck, 2002: 21). The Risk Society is characterized by decisions that are industrially produced and potentially 'politically reflexive' (Beck, 2002: 183). Beck's concern is with industrial production and ecological risk, typified by phenomena such as acid rain, global warming and Chernobyl, and with the loss of identity and heightened insecurity associated with more flexible work patterns (Beck, 1998). As he puts it, there is the 'irrepressible ubiquity of radical uncertainty in the modern world' (Beck, 1998: 10). For Beck, there are three responses to risk: denial, apathy or transformation.

Risks such as the escalating cost of water and its diminishing supply in some regions, and its excess (in flooding) in others, as a result of climate changes, may have to be factored into scenario planning. Beck makes the point that risks are events that are in the consciousness as a threat, as something that could happen. Added to this, is that a feature of the Risk Society is that risks often cannot be anticipated. Scenario planners are therefore trying to plan for the unknowable – not an easy job! To the extent that such risks are factored in, then the usefulness of scenarios increases with the realism of their assumptions. However, from a strategy perspective, the ability to manage these scenarios diminishes.

All that organizations can do is be aware of the risks and take avoiding or compensating behaviour, and try to factor these calculations into future products, markets and promotions. For instance, in the two years running up to the last millennium, many large organizations spent huge resources on preparing for the millennium bug, which, it was feared, at midnight on 31 December 1999 was going to lay waste to organizations and cripple their capacity to act. While the millennium bug proved lucrative for many IT contractors, it never materialized and we will never know whether this was because of the expensive precautions or because it was never a risk.

The millennium bug points to another feature of the Risk Society – risks are not given and out there in reality, rather they get talked into being through the media and government bodies. In this sense, some risks can take on a hysterical quality as media hype engulfs them. Beck refers to this as the 'techniques of visualization' which bring them to reality. Without this process, the risks do not exist within the consciousness of actors. Beck regards risk as being underscored by irony: the more we talk about security, the more risks occur. While risk is universal, it is often the poor that are most acutely affected – such as in the flooding of New Orleans – but this can bring about 'an involuntary demonstration' in that normally silenced voices get heard.

Risk Management

As organizations carry out their scenario studies, it is increasingly likely that they will take into account potential risks for the future. Power's thesis (2007) is that over the last decade there has been an explosion in interest in Risk Management, moving it to the centre-stage of organizational activity. And as we have already argued, if something is centre-stage, then it is by definition constituted as strategy! While Risk Management *per se* is nothing new, it has been revolutionized by the rise of the risk management industry which, as Power notes, has been successful in translating itself into a wide range of contexts (Czarniawska and Sevón, 1996). The institutional carriers of this discourse have been the major consultancies, 'the Basel Committee,

The Group of Thirty, large banks and public corporations' (Power, 2007: 190). Risk management has become a 'powerful source of normative isomorphism for all kinds of organizations, expressing a near irresistible model of rationality because it is anchored at the world-level' (Power, 2007: 193). There is an interesting paradox, however, as very often organizations will adopt highly procedural, tick-box style approaches to Risk Management which are more concerned with demonstrating that they have 'done everything reasonable' (Power, 2007: 11) than searching out risks. At least this way they will be safe in terms of the insurance claims they can make when risk materializes as crisis! In this sense, to use a phrase from Mike Power's earlier work on audits (Power, 1997), Risk Management is, perhaps, more concerned with the production of comfort to managers, stake-holders and insurance agencies than anything else. The rise of the Risk Management industry means, in effect, that Risk Management evaluates itself as a self-referential discourse.

Power (2007) argues that 'when uncertainty is organized it becomes a "risk" to be managed', an insight that leads us directly back to the stuff of strategy. If the management of risk is increasingly the stuff of organizations, then managing future risk becomes a central activity of the scenario planners. Following Beck, Power sees risk as often being created by the very tools that seek to manage and control it. The case he draws attention to is that of financial risk models used in the City, which may actually be responsible for creating financial crises.

At the time of writing this book, a new term entered the vernacular: sub-prime lending. Sub-prime lending refers to the provision of loans to people with bad credit histories and/or insecure employment. In North America it seems pretty clear that the major banks acted irresponsibly in their lending policies, giving huge loans to people who were particularly vulnerable to interest rates rises, in part because the incentive structure and key performance indicators of branch managers and front-desk personnel were structured in such a way that it made short-term financial sense for them, as organizational actors, to do so. The upshot is that there has been a huge number of people defaulting on loans – granted to them by banks – on which they can no longer afford the repayments. The reverberations of these decisions have shaken the very foundations of the banking system. The day we wrote these words, the largest US bank, Citigroup, wrote down $11 billion in bad debts attributed to the sub-prime débâcle. General liquidity has tightened as banks have had less access to inter-bank lending because other banks have been reluctant to engage in the routine banking practice of lending money to each other. The upshot of this has been a 'credit crunch' where very little money has been available to banks. For Northern Rock, a major UK mortgage provider, this has been calamitous. There was, quite literally, a run on the bank in the summer of 2007, which saw thousands of investors queuing up to withdraw their savings. On the first day alone, savers withdrew over £2 billion of their money, denoting and excacerbating the first run on a British high street bank since the Victorian period. Fearing a collapse of the banking system, the UK government pumped over £40 billion into Northern Rock to keep it afloat. The central banks of large economies are currently trying to grapple with a problem which has the potential to precipitate a major world recession. Given our warning about trying to predict the future, we are not going to make any gnomic statements in this chapter! Though this example of strategy gone bad does illustrate the very real dangers faced in the Risk Society.

conclusion

Organizations have always had to have a means of dealing with the future. Equally, each generation thinks that it is uniquely undergoing unique change. Over the last thirty years, scenario planning has emerged as a popular technique through which strategists try to envisage a range of futures for the organization. To some extent the method helps the organization engage in a reflexive exercise of understanding what the future *might* look like. While scenario planning seeks to anticipate the future, the Risk Society thesis – a popular sociological theory – suggests that the world is now defined by increased risks which cross time, space and social context. In a world of perceived heightened risks, it is perhaps no surprise that the ever resourceful management ideas industry – together with powerful banking groups – have been successful in translating a model of Risk Management throughout the corporate and government world. Uncertainty is what brings these three threads together in this chapter. Strategists planning for the future necessarily have to engage with risk. The risk is that the unforeseen may happen: think 9/11 (see Cunha et al., 2006).

6

Strategy = Emergence *and* Rational Planning

introduction

In Chapter 1, we noted the fondness for war metaphors in strategy. War, of course, has claims to be one of the fields in which many of the oldest professions thrived. However, there are other, less martial, professions. As Chandler (1962) implicitly recognized with his assertion that strategy follows structure, an adaptation of Louis Sullivan's (1988) architectural maxim that form follows function, one way in which strategy can be reframed is through using architecture and design as metaphors with which to rethink the field of strategy. In her article 'In defense of strategy as design', Jeanne Liedtka (2000) argues that the prime objective of strategy is to create a purposeful space that allows particular activities, relationships and behaviours to flourish. 'Good strategy', as well as 'good design', creates a harmonious blending of different elements that forms a whole.

Strategy as design focuses on the creation of such a harmonious system. The key to this outcome is the design process itself. For Liedtka, the design process is characterized as one of negotiation, learning and exploring opportunities as they unfold. The process is less analytical and more creative, allowing for 'trial and error' and the playful exploration of ideas. It is a perspective on strategy that is futuristic as design is fundamentally focused on shaping and forming what does not yet exist. It is future oriented and, by nature, generative.

However, putting your finger on the design attributes that are responsible for superior strategy is not so straightforward. Take the example of the two fast-food chains McDonald's and Wimpy in the UK (see Campbell and Alexander, 1997). Managers at Wimpy noticed that McDonald's restaurants were much cleaner and, since cleanliness is a decisive factor in the fast-food business, they tried to make their restaurants cleaner. Failing to raise the standard without spending lots of money, managers at Wimpy scrutinized how McDonald's achieved standards. They found out that it was the attitude of staff, using their downtime to clean the restaurant, which was important.

McDonald's clearly had a strategic advantage in respect of cleanliness. What was McDonald's strategy? Did they spend money and time to create a corporate culture that would lead to highly motivated staff? Or did they decide to create especially clean restaurants and build a corporate culture programme around it? Or did they find out that they already had motivated staff and that it would be easy to turn this into an advantage? Was cleanliness a purpose or rather an (unintended) effect of other objectives, such as developing a strong corporate culture?

The distinction between pre-planned objective and emergent results becomes blurred when we ask such questions, which is why the process of strategy-making has to be considered as being both top-down and bottom-up. Valuable insights for strategy formulation may reside in the head of the employees who implement strategy as much as in the heads of those who think (they think) it. Also, the implementation and the emerging shortcomings and insights can be the basis for tomorrow's strategy. In fact, implementation becomes a part of the strategy formulation process. The general points that are being referred to here come out clearly when we look at some of the literature on successful Japanese strategies. Japanese organizations have developed ways of building implementation into strategy and of involving rank-and-file employees in its development, even though, on the whole, they are highly bureaucratic and centralized organizations.

At the heart of the most famous Japanese corporations is a core labour force – perhaps one-fifth of the overall workforce – that is employed in a lifetime employment system. The lifetime employment system is not a formal contract but a commitment on the side of both the management and those employees to whom it is extended: those in the internal core labour market. Companies seek to maintain such workers in an employment career with the firm while workers seek to work in one company until retirement age. It is this system that enables a Japanese company to become a learning organization. The company can emphasize training, employees can be rotated to gain broad knowledge and accumulate knowledge through long years of service. In many Japanese organizations there are no job titles, wages are paid by status and the skill level determines the status grade.

These conditions make the organization more flexible, as does the fact that in the Japanese corporation flexibility is achieved at the expense of the many part-time, seasonal and sub-contract employees that the large corporations employ and retrench for flexibility.

Most successful Japanese corporations are highly centralized organizations. Centralization is convenient for making large-scale strategic moves through rational planning. The head office is large, research laboratories are centralized, and product divisions, if they are used, are not delegated overall functions as independent units. The structure of the overall organization is not as sharply defined as in the classic divisional US firm. Also, centralization is useful in developing and consolidating the core competencies of the corporation. While centralized, the organization tends to practice 'soft' domination (Courpasson, 2000) and be organic structures in which specific jobs are defined ambiguously and where group decision-making characterizes each level of the hierarchy.

Successful Japanese strategy is arrived at by consensus. Group decision-making is applied right through to the top level. The management committee meets once a week to make strategic decisions. At the middle levels of management it is normal for many meetings to be held and for committees to be formed. At the front line, quality circles provide opportunities for employees to offer ideas. The *ringi* system is employed widely, where any document for decision is reviewed by as many sections as are concerned, approved or modified, signed or stamped by each section. This system is used to confirm group decisions or to make simple decisions of less importance, meaning that implementation is less likely to become an occasion for resistance to change. Group decision-making may be time-consuming and a decision may be delayed, but implementation can be faster because the participants understand not only the decision but also the processes that produced it.

The group-decision system entails that strategy is arrived at after collecting a great deal of information and ideas and considering them from many different angles in analytical fashion. Detailed information has to be supplied in order to persuade most participants. Members share information and ideas. Because so much information is collected, the level of risk is made clear. Consequently, the decisions made often involve more risk-taking than would otherwise be the case. Additionally, responsibility is diffused. In Japan, we may say that, within the constraints of a hierarchical and centralized organization form, a relatively democratic from of strategy is practised.

One of the reasons why Japanese firms are supposed to be strategically agile and successful is that they minimize the differentiation between key roles such as R&D and production, and top management and the rest of the organization (Clegg and Kono, 2002). Where top management is symbolically situated at the top of the corporate eyrie, sometimes in another place from the bulk of organizational activity, and rarely engages with everyday life in the organization, there is every chance that errors of abstraction will compound. Rational planning requires abstraction to be successful but it also needs deep engagement.

the emergent process of strategy-making

In the western world, the idea of rational planning was increasingly questioned as an approach to strategy by a school of thought that can be described as the emergence school. Basically, this school focuses on the social and human dynamics that make strategy a powerful organizational tool. Its theorists included Cohen, March and Olsen (1972), Lindblom (1959), and Weick (1979). What they have in common is that they are all influenced by the work of the Nobel Economics prize-winner Herbert A. Simon, on decision-making. As you will remember from Chapter 2, Simon's essential insight was that when we make decisions, we never do so under conditions of perfect rationality – we always do so in conditions of more or less uncertainty and knowledge. Rather than being utterly rational optimizers, weighing every known fact and interpretation, waiting for all the evidence to be available, we operate in a 'boundedly rational' way.

The notion of bounded rationality is meant to capture the way in which organizational decisions are actually made: evidence is searched for, usually through channels of information that are known in advance. The evidence weighed is by no means exhaustive, but it is usually thorough in terms of the familiar ways of making sense that the organization and its decision-makers use. Hence, rather than seeking optimization – in an economic model of the rational consumer under conditions of perfect competition – organizations typically seek to 'satisfice', a term that Simon created to capture the process of drawing on limited but familiar channels of information to arrive at the most satisfactory decision with regard to the evidence available.

We can see how these assumptions are worked out by reference to the garbage can model that we introduced in Chapter 2. From this perspective, organizations can be viewed as collections of choices looking for problems, issues and feelings looking for decision situations in which they might be aired, solutions looking for issues to which they might be an answer, and decision-makers looking for work. In this model it is assumed that structures influence the outcomes of decisions by affecting the time pattern of the arrival of problems, choices, solutions and decision-makers, determining the allocation of organizational and individual energy and establishing linkages among the various streams of resources. As Mintzberg (1990) pointed out, high complexity and fast rates of change require emergent strategies, whereas a top-down strategy-making process is most suitable for relatively stable situations characterized by low complexity. In turbulent environments (high uncertainty), the process of defining a strategy becomes a messy and experimental process driven from the bottom up.

Strategy is more a process than a state, when viewed as emergent, as both Pettigrew's (1985) deep empirical research into ICI and Child's (2002) theoretical modelling suggested. Both researchers pointed to the importance of what Child (2002) had termed 'strategic choice' – the ways in which past strategies created path dependencies such that the subsequent paths that were taken were often dependent on decisions made in the past. As Pettigrew noted, it was power and politics that determined these decisions as much as rational analysis. This is not to say that the strategies were irrational – they were informed by rational analysis – but it was rational analysis acting as a handmaiden to powerfully embedded and contingent interests.

Building on these perspectives recently, there have been attempts to redefine static views of strategy into process-based perspectives on strategy-making. The process-based view of strategy-making 'refers to how the collective system called organization establishes, and when necessary changes, its basic orientation. Strategy-making also takes up the complex issue of collective intention – how an organization composed of many people makes up *its* mind, so to speak' (Mintzberg, 1989: 25). For instance, when top management, enclosed in boardrooms and detached from corporate everyday life, works out a seemingly perfect strategy, major problems can occur when employees have to bring this strategy into existence on a day-to-day basis. A strategy that is highly abstract and abstracted can founder on the substantive reefs of implementation. Serious concerns can be raised as to whether top management is ever likely to really know enough and have the necessary information to make sound decisions concerning strategic possibilities and impossibilities. Employees might know much more about customer needs, business operations and inimitable practices, and how to improve them, than a detached management.

making sense through strategy

Karl Weick (1979) uses an anecdote that describes this school of strategic thinking quite well because it stresses the virtues of resources being available at a specific point in time as well as opportunism in their use. As the story goes, a group of soldiers became lost in the bitterly cold and snowy Alps. Unfortunately, they didn't have any compasses or proper maps that could help them find their way out of there. By coincidence, one of them found an old map in one of his pockets. Although the map didn't represent the terrain too well, after a few wrong turns they found their way. As they returned to their camp and showed the life-saving map to their colleagues, one of them noticed that it wasn't a map of the Alps at all, but of the Pyrenees. Turned strategically, the moral of this story is quite appealing: strategies, like maps, are means of orientation, but not in a simple way that maps tell you, literally, where you are and where you should go to get where you want to be. Like the map in the story, strategies can assure people and give them confidence as well as make them think about future directions and ways of arriving there. Strategy does not give you an accurate and true picture of where you are, but it helps you to orientate yourself. It is a social construction of reality, constructing a terrain it ostensibly mirrors.

According to Karl Weick (1979), strategic planning has many important functions, although they are different from what one might assume. As Ambrose Bierce said, to plan is to 'bother about the best method of accomplishing an accidental result' (quoted in Weick, 1979: 10–11). First, it brings people together and makes them think about where they are and where they want to go. It is simply a way of addressing the future – speaking about missions and visions, hopes and fears, opportunities and threats. Strategy motivates and animates an organization. It represents an organization's dreams and, in scenario planning, a way of overcoming its worst nightmares.

Think of a high-tech company that announces its vision in big words – 'being the world's leading innovator in its market'. Regardless of whether this is realistic or not, this statement might capture the attention of young, ambitious and highly motivated scientists who hope to realize their ambitions in this company and so get hired. As a result, the company might really become an innovative enterprise. In this case, the strategic intent was realized *because* it was announced. The strategic goal was accomplished not because of a major planning effort but because of smart communication, which quite literally talked the plan into reality. This is what is referred to as self-fulfilling prophecy: the communicated plan is realized because it is communicated.

strategy as revolution

Unusual times require unusual strategies, suggests Gary Hamel (1996: 69–82), saying that 'strategy is revolution; everything else is tactics'. What matters is being unique, different and revolutionary, overturning the industrial order, being 'industry revolutionaries' (Hamel, 1996). (Perhaps it was this enthusiasm for revolution that led Hamel to endorse the Enron approach to business before its dark side became evident?) There are ten principles of 'revolutionary' strategy, according to Hamel (1996):

1 *Strategic planning may be planning but it isn't strategic*: Planning is a rational process that resembles programming, whereas strategizing is about discovering and playfully exploring the potentials for revolution.
2 *Strategy-making must be subversive*: Strategy must question the taken for granted and the conventions that inform yesterday's business and competitors' actions. Anita Roddick, founder of the Body Shop, said: 'I watch where the cosmetic industry is going and then walk in the opposite direction.'
3 *The bottleneck is at the top of the bottle*: Normally, senior managers define strategy. The normal organizational hierarchy is based on experience but in fast-changing environments, successful past experience can become the obstacle to tomorrow's success. Thus, it has to

be supplemented with a hierarchy of imagination, which might be inversely distributed compared to the formal hierarchy.

4   *Revolutionaries exist in every company*: It is a fallacy to believe that top management is pro-change whereas employees always resist. Every organization has its revolutionaries who do not sit in the front row, but they have the ability to provide fresh insights. If they don't challenge the company from the inside, they will challenge it from without in the marketplace.

5   *Change is not the problem, engagement is*: Too often 'change' is a word for routine attempts to restructure a business. However, it is more important to engage people, especially revolutionaries, in a discourse about the future and create commitment.

6   *Strategy-making must be democratic*: Instead of being a form of intellectual incest among top managers who have known each other for years and are culturally rather uniform, strategy-making must be flexible. It should include young people, outsiders and people from the margins, as they develop views that are normally unseen and unheard. They don't conform to an organization's orthodoxy and thus can provide truly revolutionary insights.

7   *Anyone can be a strategy activist*: Revolutionaries are never on the top of a hierarchy – they are spread throughout the entire organizations. Giving them a voice and providing them with space to speak means transforming their anarchistic potential into activist energy.

8   *Perspective is worth 50 IQ points*: It's not easy to make people smarter, but one can provide new glasses through which the world looks different. Change of perspective leads to shifts in the things that an organization sees, which, implicitly, makes new opportunities visible.

9   *Top-down and bottom-up are not the alternatives*: It is not either/or but a question of organizing communication between people who have responsibility and expertise and people who have fantasy and engagement.

10 *You cannot see the end from the beginning*: Open-ended strategy-making processes lead to surprises. The new cannot be judged on the premises of the old because it follows different rules. Moreover, a really open process leads to a future that cannot be predicted as it unfolds because people explore new avenues.

Hamel is not the only strategy revolutionary. The most famous is Tom Peters, who has advanced the cause of 'Cultural Revolution' in management. Along with Michael Porter, Peters would be one of the most influential strategy gurus on the planet. Yet, it is surprising where his inspiration seems to have come from. Unlikely resonances occur as ideas travel (Czarniawska and Sevón, 1996). The idea of 'cultural revolution' began in Beijing and travelled widely through China, but it did not end there. It had resonances in European universities in the 1960s. Surprisingly, it also had resonances in American and other business schools from the 1980s onwards. The last place one might expect to find enthusiasm for 'cultural revolution' is in management theory. However, there are many echoes. Consider the importance that Peters attaches to culture, the crucial need of attacking 'old' things and the critical success formula attached to implementing 'new' things. All of these are recipes that could have come directly from Mao's Cultural Revolution.

Tom Peters proselytizes constant revolutionary change in *Re-imagine! Scorecard and Revolution Planner* (http:www.tompeters.com/slides/uploaded/Re-imagine_scorecard/html) and treats such a revolutionary approach as a process for sudden intuitive leaps of understanding, or epiphany, to combat the hardening of metaphorically managerial arteries in bureaucratic structures. In a consulting scenario, organizational members often face an attempt by consultants to impose a new social hegemony (Gramsci, 1971). These strategies are marked by the use of binary categorization devices targeted at disestablishing dominant power and bureaucracies. Such a process of articulation of discursive categories is subject to renegotiation and a contestation of meaning.

---

tompeters!company website

tompeters!company is Tom Peters' management consulting and training firm founded in Palo Alto, California, in 1984, and now operating internationally from hubs in Boston, London, and Manchester, Vermont.

Our client work typically involves applying one or more of Tom's core strategies to a specific business context.

Our style is what you would expect from Tom's brand: provocative, high-energy, and having a strong bias for action!

Our client promise? Custom solutions! Innovation, energy, and change! Top team alignment! Projects with real impact! Great leadership! High-performing professionals and business teams! Engaged people who embrace change!

We deploy our Intellectual Property from an evolving blend of talented and committed people, insightful diagnostic tools, and powerful implementation systems. In short, Re-imagined business excellence! ....

Be distinct ... or extinct!

*http://tompeterscompany.com/

The major 'Intellectual Property' of the tompeters!company is the *Re-imagine! Scorecard and Revolution Planner*. It is a tool of 'Cultural Revolution' for management. In many of his presentations to large business groups, and in his book *Re-imagine!* (2003), Peters accentuates a 'them and us' mentality. The dualism is presented as an imperative to managers to unleash organizational change programmes with which to pursue a witch hunt within their organizations. The whole emphasis stresses that managers should seek out and label what are the old and smash them – 'out with the old' and 'in with the new': new work context, new technology, new organization, new customers, new markets, new work, new people, new management.

Tom Peters was a consultant for McKinsey, based in the San Francisco office and connected to Stanford University. In 1977, Peters was directed to lead a project on organization structure and people. Peters travelled the world on an expansive budget, with the brief of talking to as many interesting business people he could find, about teams and organizations in business.

> In 1979 McKinsey's Munich office requested Peters to present his findings to Siemens, which provided the spur for Peters to create a 700-slide, two-day presentation. Word of the meeting reached the US and Peters was invited to present also to PepsiCo, but unlike the hyper-organized Siemens, the PepsiCo management required a tighter format than 700 slides, so Peters produced eight themes. (http://www.businessballs.com/tompetersinsearchofexcellence.htm)

The eight themes were produced with a fair leavening of what he had learnt at Stanford, as Colville et al. (1999) record: the intellectual traces of Weick and March were discernible. Consultants engage in sensemaking (Weick, 1995), legitimacy creation (Suchman, 1995), and the dissemination of isomorphic routines and practices (DiMaggio and Powell, 1983/2002). Through such processes, consultants overtly or implicitly label particular organizational practices as 'normal' or 'ideal' and others as 'abnormal' or 'undesirable' and then proceed to 'cure' the organization of its abnormalities.

Peters drew on influential and unconventional ideas that have more recent echoes. It has been noted that unpredictability does not imply the absence of order while recurrence does not exclude novelty (Tsoukas, 1998). Similarly, Mintzberg alerted us to two dangers that organizations face: the danger of imploding and exploding. Mintzberg (1989: 365) argues that 'every form of organization sows the seeds of its own destruction' (also see Schumpeter, 1954). For, as Weick (1979: 189) writes: 'The inability of people in organizations to tolerate equivocal processing may well be one of the most important reasons why they have trouble. ... It is the unwillingness to disrupt order, ironically, that makes it impossible for the organization to create order.' In this dialectic, it is the attempt to create order though planning that causes chaos in the first place. Paradoxically, letting things evolve more freely might lead to a more stable situation. Think of a high-wire performer: she is moving constantly in order to keep her balance and stay up in the air. Paradoxically, movement equals stability (see Clegg et al., 2005).

Perversely, in the name of rebellion and resistance, cultural revolutionaries such as Peters demand total commitment by members in their organization and the subsumption of their identity to that of being an organization member *in toto*. He wants to overthrow bureaucracy both substantively and in principle. Bureaucracy should be replaced with a new kind of total institution in which energized team members commit themselves wholly to the goals of the organization.

In order to give shape to the struggle against bureaucracy, Peters identifies it with a specific reactionary figure and ethos. The figure is Robert McNamara and the ethos is that of the Harvard Business School. Peters is on frequent record as saying that his whole life has been a struggle against the legacy of Robert McNamara, which he saw as having become the essential *de facto* wisdom of the Harvard Business School, setting the pace for large American enterprise in the post-war era. 'Start with Taylorism, add a layer of Druckerism and a dose of McNamaraism, and by the late 1970s you had the great American corporation that was being run by bean counters' (http://www.businessballs.com/tompetersinsearchofexcellence. htm). The enemy is clearly the long-range planning model of strategy personified and institutionalized.

The prescriptions that Peters dispenses often lead to downsizing and layoffs. Louis Uchitelle, in his book *The Disposable American: Layoffs and Their Consequences* (2006), regards extensive layoffs as the tangible outcome of the cultural revolutionary message as preached by consultants such as Peters. Layoffs hollow out companies, middle-class jobs and

American dreams. Employees who are laid off often drop permanently to a demeaning, low-wage way of life, transforming work in America. Over 30 million full-time American employees have been laid off since 1984 (when the systematic record-keeping began). But Uchitelle says we should also include early retirees who could see what was going to happen to them. These contemporary layoffs almost never work again in comparably salaried jobs, but join the ranks of a low-wage economy, helping create the kind of labour market flexibility that we have seen in Japan. Uchitelle denies that downsizing makes for more productive, more competitive, more flexible organizations: with fewer employees many organizations lose resilience and innovation suffers. Costs are cut rather than innovations fostered. In 2004, more than 45 per cent of American workers were earning $13.25 an hour or less. The jobs that the country has been 'growing' the fastest include those such as janitor, hospital orderly and check-out operative rather than the skilled jobs that are being lost.

Uchitelle is baffled by the collapse of any serious resistance to these mass layoffs, which he attributes to the personalized and individualized accounts of them that those laid off use to make sense of their plight. They have taken on the categorization devices of those who made them redundant. Stein (2001) argues that the categorization devices used to describe the destruction of jobs and livelihoods represent a systematic assault on meaning. Terms such as 'downsizing', 'rightsizing' and 'de-bureaucratization' not only conceal the cruel nature of many current organizational practices, but also naturalize political decisions as if they were the natural logic of institutions such as markets, economic necessity and shareholder value. Consultants such as Peters can thus be seen as the voice of reason against embedded hierarchies and privileges. Stein sees emotional brutality, symbolic violence, dehumanization, degradation, humiliation and intimidation as the norm for organizations subject to Cultural Revolution.

conclusion

Strategists do not just advise on strategy; they talk strategy, and its effects, into being. Peters does not destroy things in quite the same way that the Chinese Cultural Revolutionaries did. What he, and others who have drawn inspiration from his ideas, destroy are institutions and organizations. Kallinikos (2006) captures the thinking behind the revolutionary slogans very clearly. While bureaucracy may be seen as too inward-looking, too concerned with its own procedures, with doing things according to rule, this critique 'understates the fact that extreme concern with external contingencies and adaptability in the long run hollows outs social systems (as they hollow out individuals) from the inside' (Kallinikos, 2006: 141). These hollow men and women of the corporation will, ideally, be driven wholly by events, by contingent demands and their commitment and involvement in responding to them. Hollowed-out men and women, following the enthusiasms of the moment, as these are filtered through the convictions of their leaders and which they are supposed to enact with trust, as empowered and totally committed individuals, begin to look worryingly like the inmates of total institutions constructed as prisons of commitment (see Clegg et al., 2006: Chapter 6). Nonetheless, as Kallinikos (2006: 145–6) suggests, they increasingly people the scenarios of contemporary strategic HRM, a vocational discourse that targets the individual as a 'psychological unity', seeking to minimize the friction between the character of the person and the needs of the roles that they fulfil organizationally, allowing the expansion of work and professional concerns into the lifeworld that was once held secure outside the role of the organization. At its core, the new cultural revolutionaries seek a totalizing creep into and envelopment of an increasing part of the organizational members' lifeworld, in a manner that it is difficult to see as other than corrosive or destructive.

7

Strategy is What Strategists Do!
Strategy as Practice

▨▨▨ introduction

Strategy is supposed to lead an organization through changes and shifts to secure its future growth and sustainable success. Strategy has become the master concept with which to address CEOs of contemporary organizations and their senior managers. Its talismanic importance can hardly be overstated. Thus, as we have seen, strategic management is increasingly understood as *the* task of the top-management team. However, as we have seen in earlier chapters, there is more to strategy than a senior management team scanning the environment, devising a strategy, and then implementing it. Of course, many strategists think this is what they do, but it is a form of illusion – even delusion – to think so because it ignores the fact that strategists often have limited room for manoeuvre, and while their strategies will have all sorts of consequences, these will not necessarily be those that they intended.

▨▨▨ the 'strategy as practice' approach

In recent years a new approach to strategy has emerged. It has its origins in European management schools (Jarzabowski, 2003; Samra-Fredericks, 2003; Whittington, 2004) and is best understood as a critique of orthodox, hegemonic and mainly North American, or North American-inspired, strategy research. Most strategy research in North America is dominated by industrial economics with its very positivistic mindset. Invariably, the research conducted involves running regressions and econometric models on very large datasets, from which generalizable rules are constructed. Such an approach to strategy has many problems: how can a 'rule' be generalized across time, space and context? This does not deter strategists operating in this frame. We think they are suffering from a medical affliction that Bent Flyvbjerg (2001) has termed 'physics envy'. One of the symptoms of physics envy is to treat the social world – made up of human beings going about their business – as if it were the same as the physical world. Put simply, we are far from convinced that the social world can be modelled in the way in which a law of gravity, for instance, can be proposed, tested and proved. One of the ironies of such an approach is that it writes out the role of the strategists – it does not analyze their agency – which seems to undermine the whole premise of strategy!

The new approach, known as 'strategy as practice' (S-A-P), tries to write the role of the strategist back into analysis. Some of its important foundational texts include Balogun and Johnson (2004), Jarzabowski (2003, 2004), Johnson, Melin and Whittington (2003) and Whittington (2004). In this book we have argued that many strategy ideas are overly simple or that they ignore the complex nature of organizations. Over the last seven years or so, a network of strategy scholars in different universities but with a somewhat shared agenda of interests – an 'action net', to use Barbara Czarniawska's (2002) felicitous phrase – has been constructed that has led to the emergence and partial institutionalization of a 'strategy as practice' group. It draws on several diverse currents to form its perspective, as we illustrate on pages 99–100.

At the core of S-A-P is a concern for what strategic actors actually do and the kinds of activity they carry out when they strategize (Hendry, 2000; Jarzabowski, 2003; Johnson et al., 2003; Whittington, 1996, 2002). Accordingly, the practice-based approach investigates the nitty-gritty details of strategy formation – the routines of budgeting, the expenditure meetings, the reports and presentations, etc. – through focusing on 'praxis, practitioners and practices' (Whittington, 2002). Similarly, Johnson et al. (2003: 14) argue that it is 'time to shift the strategy research agenda towards the micro'. In 2003, Richard Whittington, a professor at Oxford University and one of the prime movers of the S-A-P movement, outlined a vision of

New directions in strategy research

Topics	Authors	Themes
How power and politics shape the strategies that emerge	Mintzberg (1987); Pettigrew (1973, 1985); Pettigrew and Whipp (1991); Van de Ven (1992)	A focus on emergence, on strategy as a sense that is made by strategists of what they are doing as they are doing it. The contrast is with strategy as a rational planned process that is first developed and then implemented. In these perspectives, strategy is much more organic, spontaneous and less explicitly causal and rational.
Strategic choices made to focus on some things and not others	Child (2002)	Strategy is what top-management teams – or dominant coalitions – do. They will choose to focus on some contingencies rather than others. For instance, they may seek to manage the size of the enterprise – often a key consideration for family-owned businesses that do not want to lose control – or they may choose to try to manage the environment – perhaps by colluding with competitors in price-fixing.
The language games which constitute strategy	Barry and Elmes (1997); Heracleous and Barrett (2001); Knights and Morgan (1991)	Strategy is what strategists say. What strategists do is use the language of strategy. Talking the talk is a way of showing linguistic competence as a *bona fide* strategist. Strategy can be studied through attending, closely and carefully, to the discourse of strategy in written and spoken texts. Strategy produces subject positions, such as 'the strategist' and those who are the subjects – and the objects – of strategy.
Interpretative approaches to understanding strategy	Chaffee (1985); Schwenk (1989); De La Ville and Mounoud (2003)	In his interpretive strategic model, Chaffee (1985: 93) argues that organizations are 'a collection of social agreements entered into by

(Continued)

(Continued)

Topics	Authors	Themes
		individuals of free will' with the aim to 'attract enough individuals to cooperate in mutually beneficial exchange', and can deal with complexity. From this perspective, strategy is based on a social contract and organizational reality is based on the socially defined reality that people construct. Logically, the interpretative strategic model puts an emphasis on communication, symbols and shared meaning.
Strategy seen through structuration theory	Whittington (1992)	Strategy is constrained by pre-existing sets of relations, which are referred to as structure. Yet, the essence of strategy is the exercise of agency – of people trying to get things done. The relation of structure to agency is problematic. In this approach, it is seen to be resolved through agents drawing on the rules and resources of structures, which constrain their actions, to try to achieve strategic agendas. Agents cannot choose strategy freely; they inhabit a history against which they struggle.

strategy which built on the new concerns that sought to do precisely this by posing a series of questions as an agenda for strategy to address:

- 'Where and how is the work of strategizing and organizing actually done?'
- 'Who does this strategizing and organizing work?'
- 'What are the skills for this work and how are they acquired?'
- 'What are the common tools and techniques of strategizing and organizing?'
- 'How is the work of strategizing and organizing done?'
- 'How are the products of strategizing and organizing communicated and consumed?'

Whittington's objectives are to treat strategy as an important social practice, which means that we need to investigate those who make up strategy, who do strategizing – the strategists – and understand how they make decisions that have important effects on the rest of us. Knowledge of these practices should help improve strategy by creating more reflexive strategists. 'Reflexivity', as the word suggests, is supposed to enable people – in this case the strategists – to be reflective about how their actions are possible and thus to understand their activities as strategists in relation to those assumptions that make their strategy work possible. Whittington and his colleagues (Whittington, 2004) highlight a concern with heightening levels of reflexivity among strategists, embarking on a programme of reform of strategy among both the practitioner and academic communities (Cummings, 2003). In its short history, the S-A-P approach has made quite a splash by using 'the practice label [to] give coherence to a range of existing streams of research' (Whittington, 1996: 734). Given the claims S-A-P makes for itself, it is worth examining the approach critically. In the sections below we will look at the approach's relation to the concept of strategy and will analyze the concept of practice utilized.

the concept of 'strategy' in the 'strategy as practice' approach

The notion of strategy developed by the 'strategy as practice' approach depicts strategy as an activity: 'strategy' is not only an attribute of firms but also an *activity undertaken by people*. Strategy is something people *do* (Jarzabowski, 2004: 529). Jarzabowski's empirical study (2003: 35) focuses on the strategic achievement of the balance that universities attain when they 'gain "strength" through strong leadership combined with excellent performance in research ranking and income-generation, so maintaining power in their relationships with the centre'. So what is new about this conceptualization of strategy? Such a description of power balances is based on traditional strategy themes, including strong leadership and excellent performance, coupled with a resource-dependence perspective familiar from Salancik and Pfeffer's (1974) university study. It is difficult to see what Jarzabowski offers that is new. The quote below illustrates the conservatism of her definition:

> Key strategic practices are identified as those formal operating
> procedures involved in the direction setting, resource allocation, and
> monitoring and control. While these are not the only practices from
> which strategic action is constructed, they are theoretically valid
> within the strategic management literature and are innately 'practical',
> being concerned with the doing of strategy. (Jarzabowski, 2003: 23)

The S-A-P approach has an ambiguous relationship with well-established conservative notions of strategy more generally. For instance, Johnson et al. (2003: 6) regard the resource-based view (RBV) as particularly relevant. They argue that their micro-perspective is able to improve on some of these weaknesses of RBV through 'the value generated' by looking closely at 'the seeming minutiae of organizations, at the periphery as well as the centre' (Johnson et al., 2003: 6). The fondness for RBV is curious. The RBV bears the imprint of its industrial economics origins and, while it is unclear what it has to offer S-A-P, the intellectual straitjacket it places on the intellectual development of the new perspective is very clear. Paradigmatically speaking, the alliance with RBV makes no sense at all. That this is so is evident from work by David Knights (2002), which challenges strategy thinkers to break away from extant economic metaphors that condemn us to very limited and particular conversations (see also Czarniawska, 2005).

Whereas the references to RVB remain unclear, it is interesting to note that consideration of key strategists, such as Mintzberg, are absent from the 'strategy as practice' debate. Considering his work on practice and strategy, one has to wonder about this silence. For instance, as Johnson et al. (2003: 14) argue, 'our position is distinct in that it comes at the enduring issues of strategy from the bottom up'. Such an approach to strategy as bottom-up is clearly linked to Mintzberg's work on emerging strategy.

For Whittington, 'strategy as practice enables both illumination of a significant phenomenon that has hitherto been obscure and improvement of something which people personally, and society in general, have a great deal at stake' (2004: 63). We would agree with this sentiment that strategy can have important consequences for society and, as such, should be taken seriously by those who have an interest in civil society. Following this reflexive approach, strategy as practice concerns both managers who strategize and those whose possible field of action might be governed by those strategies. However, most publications in the S-A-P area start from premises that share a more managerial perspective. For instance, Johnson et al. (2003: 12) argue that 'the challenge … will be to transform descriptive contributions into more helpful models of managing'. Based on questions like 'Just what do managers have to do to make a difference and what is their impact? [and] What works for them and what does not work?' (Johnson et al., 2003: 16), the S-A-P approach remains within the tradition of mainstream, functional research. In fact, Johnson and his colleagues argue that a major justification for the S-A-P approach is that managers are 'more demanding in terms of their expectations from business schools' (Johnson et al., 2003: 5) than was the case at the outset of the strategy discourse. Therefore, there is a 'strong instrumental reason' for the S-A-P approach: it makes more sense to practitioners than the older approaches. Thus, the deliverables of the old and the new approach are the same – they claim to help managers manage better.

Not surprisingly, strategy as practice focuses on top-management teams as the locus of strategizing. For instance, as Jarzabowski (2003: 31) argues, 'The central analytic question examined *how* top teams *do* strategy in UK universities', not how is it possible that they do what it is they do, nor what constitutes these 'top teams' and allows them to call their activities strategic. From an epistemological point of view, the 'strategy as practice' approach seems to understand practice as being 'closer' to reality and delivering a 'more accurate' description of the real world than attending to the reconstructed logic of formal strategy outcomes. For Johnson et al. (2003: 15), the 'research agenda matches the lived world of organizational actors', aiming to 'build theories with greater leverage in the real world' (2003: 13). The questions that Johnson et al. (2003: 12) envisage being solved include: 'does it really help managers in their daily strategizing activities – for instance, how to run a strategy meeting or engage in everyday strategic debate in a convincing and motivating manner'. Intentionally or not, the 'strategy as practice' approach positions itself as a problem-solving tool for managerial elites. It does not emphasize the ways in which outsiders, renegades and strangers might influence strategy in practice (see for instance, Hamel, 1996). Hence, by focusing on the current elite, the approach is implicitly conservative.

the concept of 'practice' in the 'strategy as practice' approach

The 'strategy as practice' approach claims to open up a new view on strategy by engaging with the making of strategy as an outcome fashioned out of the doing of detailed work. It trades off an unease regarding the difference between the existing *theory* of what people do and what people *actually* do. In so doing, the practice approach follows what the best organizational theory has been analyzing for the last 40 years: what it is that managers actually do when they manage.

Ethnomethodological researchers have had a longstanding interest in practice (Garfinkel, 1967; Silverman and Jones, 1976). There have also been many mainstream auspices. For example, Lindblom (1968) analyzed managerial behaviour as muddling through. Starbuck (1983) found a gap between talk, action and decision in organizations, showing that on a practice level managers actually do different things than on a discursive level. Brunsson (1985) identified the useful needs of this gap for the practice of organizational hypocrisy. Mintzberg (1973) studied the daily routines of five managers and found that their roles were far more fragmented in practice than theories of rational behaviour would suggest. These researchers looked, implicitly or explicitly, at practices. In this respect, the practice approach has a long tradition that it can draw upon. It would seem that the claims for newness made by S-A-P hinder it from engaging with this pre-existing body of literature. Here, S-A-P is missing an opportunity as it could improve its concept of practice significantly by situating *and* differentiating itself from this literature.

Analyzing S-A-P, it becomes clear that the concept of practice is not defined clearly. For instance, in her 2004 article Jarzabowski differentiates between practice and practices: 'Practice is the actual activity, events, or work of strategy, while practices are those traditions, norms, rules and routines through which the work of strategy is constructed' (Jarzabowski, 2004: 545). In so doing, practice looks similar to action whereas practices become the formal procedures of organizations. Beside the rather confusing fact that the singular and the plural of the word 'practice' mean different things, practice is modelled according to the agency and structure issue at the core of structuration theory – the highly influential social theory developed by Anthony Giddens

(1984). Jarzabowski goes on to identify two key themes from structuration theory: recursiveness and adaptation. Adding to the theoretical melange, Jarzabowski (2004) draws on three additional theories to
understand practice, including *habitus*, social becoming and communities of practice. Jarzabowski then argues (2004: 531) that practice is
a 'particular type of self-reinforcing learning akin to single loop or
exploitative learning theories'. In order to become a 'practice', some
action needs to resemble a routine: 'The term "practice" implies repet-
itive performance in order to become practised; that is, to attain recurrent, habitual, or routinized accomplishments of particular actions'
(Jarzabowski, 2004: 531). Practice explains how agency and structure
are linked with each other: '... interaction between agents and socially
produced structures occurs through recursively situated practices that
form part of daily routines' (Jarzabowski, 2004: 531).

Practice as well as explaining routines has yet more weight to bear.
At the same time, practice is responsible for change and adaptation:
'Changing practice is carried out within micro-contexts in interaction
with macro-contexts. There is thus an ongoing process of social becoming that is realized through a chain of social events, or practice'
(Jarzabowski, 2004: 535). While some practice resembles routines, it
can also be a non-routinized becoming that is enacted in singular, non-
reoccurring events.

The key concept of practice is defined in a contradictory and
highly confusing way. Practice can mean anything: from routine, to
event, from becoming, to structuration theory, from learning in
macro-contexts, and thus, in the process (or one might say 'practice'), becoming a concept that can explain almost everything. One
talismanic category – strategy – is replaced with another – practice.
In practice (to pun a little), the theorizing is somewhat promiscu-
ous. Jarzabowski (2004) links the S-A-P approach back to the
resource-based view of the firm. As she puts it, the 'concept of localized practice is present in the resource-based view (RBV), which
posits that localized and hence distinctive strategic contexts are
value creating' (Jarzabowski, 2004: 537). One paragraph later,
Jarzabowski links practice to dynamic capability theory (Teece
et al., 1997). For her, the concept of 'new resource configuration'
equals adaptive practice. Moreover, the concept of practice is also the
appropriate solution for organizations in competitive environments:

'While recursive forms of practice may be appropriate under stable compet tion, hyper-competitive markets characterized by disruptive technologies and high product obsolescence requires continuous adaptation in order to create new markets' (Jarzabowski, 2004: 542). Finally, when Jarzabowski discusses the 'adoption of a practice' (2004: 547) by firms, practice is understood as a commodity (Total Quality Management, for instance) that can be transferred from one to the other company.

While none of the definitions above is wrong *per se*, we argue that they are incompatible when put together. Rather than deriving a sophisticated practice concept from social theorists such as Garfinkel (1967), Foucault (1977) or Bourdieu (1990), the S-A-P approach has adopted an unclear and contradictory definition of practice. In fact, practice can mean a myriad of things, including events, routines, rules, or simply 'being closer to reality' and 'being more practical'. As Elena Antonacopoulou (2007: 1292) has written, 'the richness in perspectives informing social practice theory could also account for the lack of clarity concerning practice'. The recruitment of scholars as diverse as Bourdieu (1977, 1990), de Certeau (1984), Foucault (1977), Giddens (1984) and Schatzki et al. (2001) to strategy as practice once again raises the question of what is its *distinctive* contribution. These theorists are well known within organization studies, and authors such as Foucault have had an enormous impact on the field. We are not convinced that the insights from these authors have been used in other than a highly ornamental way. These theorists have a certain rigour, a certain internal consistency, a complex and intellectually embedded 'style' that they wear neither as a cloak to be lightly cast off and assumed easily by a passer-by, nor as a suit of many colours into which their disparate ideas can be assembled, as an eclectic patchwork at once both disharmonious and disconcerting.

process or practice?

The ambiguity of the practice concept becomes problematic when one compares it with earlier process-based analyses of strategy. Whittington (1996: 732) states that:

Since the 1980s process researchers have been exploring how organizations come first to recognize the need for strategic change and then actually to achieve it … the practice approach draws on many insights of the process school, but returns to the managerial level, concerned with how strategists 'strategize'.

Andrew Pettigrew (1985, 1997) was pivotal in developing the processual perspective, most notably though his seminal study of strategic change at ICI. However, as Johnson et al. (2003: 13) argue, 'the agenda for the micro strategy and strategizing perspective is set by the limitations against which the process tradition has run'. As they see it, the relationship between practice and process must be imagined as follows: quoting Brown and Duguid (2000), they argue that 'practice is what is inside the process' (Johnson et al., 2003: 11). Leaving aside the methodological challenges involved in observing a practice inside a process, the critique of the practice approach is that the 'process literature is still insufficiently sensitive to the micro' (Johnson et al., 2003: 5). It doesn't go far enough into the 'blackbox' of strategizing. The 'new' approach 'should get much closer to the detailed activities that go on inside organizational processes' (Johnson et al., 2003: 13), such that 'we need to get off our verandas and get a good deal closer to the actual work that makes up the organizational systems and processes of the process tradition' (Johnson et al., 2003: 12).

From our perspective, there are three issues with this approach:

1 Theoretically, the concepts of process and practice are used interchangeably. For instance, in the same paper, Johnson et al. (2003: 3) argue for an 'activity-based view of strategy that focuses on the detailed processes and practices which constitute the day-to-day activities of organizational life and which relate to strategic outcomes'.

2 One could question whether the empirical research done by 'strategy as practice' scholars has so far developed new insights into the work of strategizing as practice. For instance, Jarzabowski's analysis of strategy as practice at Warwick University (2003) does not offer any detailed explanations of the actual practice of strategy. She focuses on the top-management team, instead of analyzing the doubtless more complex network of actors, mediators and translators involved in strategy as practice. Also, there is no mention of artefacts or details of the actual practice of strategy-making. Moreover, the focus of the research is on formal procedures rather than on emerging or

spontaneous initiatives. In fact, the organization is presented as a perfectly running machine since the 'analysis of actions from 1992 to 1998 indicates that they are consistent with the plan' (Jarzabowski, 2003: 35). Given the interest in the 'micro' aspects of everyday organizational life, such a statement can barely pass as an analysis of practices. In fact, even an economist would allow reality to diverge from plans over a six-year period.

3   In their comparison of processual research with the 'strategy as practice approach', Ezzamel and Willmott (2004) highlight key differences in their treatment of power and politics. Rather than viewing the S-A-P approach as a development of earlier processual work, they describe it as a regressive movement. Their rationale is that the processual view was sensitive to issues of power and politics, whereas by descending into the detail of managerial techniques the 'strategy as practice' approach lost its capacity to analyze power as effectively. Such an analysis requires attention to the intersection of power practices with specific forms of knowledge shaping organizational relations and techniques, as Clegg et al. (2006) argue.

extending strategy as practice to the study of things that are not done

We think that the agenda of strategy as practice can be extended quite easily and productively by bringing in a clear agenda that was sketched a long time ago. In an influential discussion, two American political scientists, Peter Bachrach and Morton Baratz (1962, 1970), discussed the politics of non-decision-making as the second face of power. The first face concerns the outcomes of decisive battles between different actors over specific issues, when an A gets a B to do something that B would not otherwise do. The second face is subtler: *non-decision-making occurs when actors systematically do not attend to a phenomenon of which they have every reason to be cognizant.* For reasons of organizationally structured 'mobilization of bias' (Schattschneider, 1960: 71), their non-attention results in 'non-decision-making'. The mobilization of bias is something that is deeply embedded in all organizations; they will have ways of formally and informally enacting the salience of phenomena that could be constituted as within their purview, and these will determine both what will be enacted and what it will be enacted to be – and not be. *From this perspective, it is not so much strategy as practice that is important but strategy as that which is not practised, not mobilized.* Some things will never make the strategy agenda as it is defined by dominant parties. They are, either implicitly or explicitly, ruled out of bounds; hence they are not raised. To adapt Haugaard's (2003: 94) terms, in such situations existing strategic elites do not collaborate in the reproduction of some issues as phenomena to be taken seriously. Only those issues that conform to the dominant myths, rituals and institutions of the strategies that they promulgate will be admitted. Hence, important issues that challenge these dominant ideas will not be acknowledged and their exclusion from consideration signals the neglected face of power.

Yet, as the changing agenda of ecological sustainability shows, resistance to ideas once seemingly immutable can come from unlikely quarters, and messages once associated with resistant radicals and considered unacceptable for the serious business of strategy work have interesting ways of metamorphosing. Strategy is done not just by doing things but also by not doing things: strategy, above all, should be considered as politics. In politics it is the non-practices – as much as the practices – that make a difference. There are always actors outside strategy's circuits who work the strategic arena, challenging, changing and metamorphosing ideas that can travel fast and far. Increasingly, the challenges that strategists will have to face are more likely to come from the practices of some extra-organizational actors – perhaps a local community or NGO movement – than from the algorithms, metaphorical diamonds and 2×2 tables of the strategists.

If analysis is restricted merely to those issues which elites sanction and officially formulate, and we do not attend to those informal mechanisms for resisting these accounts, we will miss the ways in which organizational power relations seek to restrict agendas to dominant mobilizations of bias (Friedrich, 1937). What is left unsaid in accounts positioned as legitimate, official and authoritatively formulated is sometimes more important than what is carefully articulated.

conclusion

As Whittington (2007) notes in a piece in *Organization Studies*, the time has come for S-A-P approaches to mature. We agree. The approach stands at a crossroads. It can invest in heavily branded social theory and continue to accumulate all the currently fashionable names under its roof, without regard for matters of stylistic cohesion, or it can decide what its signature is really going to be, and then work the theme systematically. And this means shaking off the slough of strategy as something done only by strategists, only when they are explicitly doing strategy; it also requires addressing what they do not do, the claims made that remain non-issues. At present the approach resembles unfocused, albeit fashionable, consumption in which, despite the attractions of the individual pieces, the collection as a whole lacks thematic unity. Strategy is irremediably political. For this reason, far more attention needs to be paid to the politics of practice in an *œuvre* somewhat more theoretically coherent yet no less entrepreneurial institutionally. The approach needs extending to incorporate the politics of non-decision-making and the politics of excluded actors who seek to change the strategic agenda. We can see some instances of why this is important quite clearly when we return to the field of war, the spiritual heartland of strategy. In fields as diverse as Vietnam, Iraq and Afghanistan, we can see that even the most powerful forces are capable of being challenged by, and have to come to an accommodation with, external agencies that are far less strategically sophisticated. It is evident that the strategy in each case was to wage war on the strategists' chosen terrain. However, the defeat of this strategy was achieved by the enemy choosing not to fight on that terrain and with those strategies, but to turn the enemies' strengths into weaknesses and to make strengths of their weaknesses. Hence, in strategy, we have to look not just at the practices of the strategic actors but also the strategies of those they come up against. In business, this might mean studying the whole field of competition – as Porter recommends. However, closer to the concerns of strategy as practice, it might mean that we should look at the ways in which social movements, activists and other 'weak' external actors manage to act as guerrillas, changing the issues and the terrain of competitive strategy in consequence. The best example of this is the way that green activism has been transformed from a stance seen as largely anti-capitalist and anti-business into a set of concerns that business has been obliged to deal with – if only, sometimes, in a more ceremonial than real way.

8

Gaps, Rhetoric and Realities

Strategists love to identify gaps but this is a technique that can be used to turn the tables on strategists themselves. If we take the mainstream of strategy to have been the rational planning model that was first framed by Ansoff, in reflection on the discourse that subsequently developed we can identify seven fallacies in the mainstream of strategic planning. We constitute these fallacies in the form of seven gaps:

1 The gap between managerial fantasy and organizational capabilities.
2 The gap between actual, clear goals and possible, unpredictable futures.
3 The gap between planning and implementing.
4 The gap between planned change and emerging evolution.
5 The gap between means and ends.
6 The gap between a planning head (management) and a planned body (organization).
7 The gap between order and disorder.

Far from managing these gaps, strategic planning actively generates and sustains them. The practice of strategic planning is what initially constitutes these gaps. It actively creates a system of divisions that constantly undermines and subverts the order that the strategic plan proposes. It is this congenital subversion that incessantly *de-* and *re-*constructs the logic of the plan, such that the innermost essence of strategic planning constantly erodes the order it promises to impose. Thinking and managing beyond such strategic practice is inspired by Cartesian logic, which is an exercise that constantly undermines itself, and hence the entire organization. It must be conceptualized in terms of a strategy whose practice frequently undercuts its assumptions. We will return to this point after briefly describing the seven fallacies of strategic thinking.

▰▰▰ The seven gaps

First, there is the gap between managerial fantasy and organizational capabilities. As Bartlett and Ghoshal (1989: 187) pointed out, organizations are captured in a 'strategic trap': 'The problem is that their [manager's] companies are organizationally incapable of carrying out the sophisticated strategies they have developed. Over the past 20 years, strategic thinking has far outdistanced organizational capabilities.' The plan promises perfect futures at the expense of imperfect presents: the plan is always a negative diagnosis of today's reality; it describes the actual situation as a deficiency, an imperfection, as negative, as a lack of something or other, in order to promise a better, utopian future. Thus strategic thinking generates a gap between unattainable futures and a more or less negative reality that should be overcome as soon as possible. It produces dissatisfaction and enhances the all too human urge to escape from the present in which we dwell rather than understanding, exploring and exploiting its manifold possibilities.

A second gap occurs between actual, clear goals and possible, unpredictable futures. Identifying a goal and deducing a strategy from it therefore means, first and foremost, to make a decision: as Porter (1996: 63) says, 'Strategy ... requires hard choices'. The concept of rational decision-making embodied in strategic planning, based on stable and clear future goals, is challenged by what Derrida calls 'undecidability':

> The undecidable is not merely the oscillation or the tension between two decisions; it is the experience of that which, though heterogeneous, foreign to the order of the calculable and the rule, is still obliged – it is an obligation that we must speak – to give itself up to the impossible decision, while taking account of law and rules. A decision that didn't go through the ordeal of the undecidable would not be a free decision; it would only be the programmable application or unfolding of a calculable process. ... [T]he

ordeal of the undecidability that I just said must be gone through by any decision worthy of the name is never past or passed, it is not a surmounted or sublated (*aufgehoben*) moment in decision. The undecidable remains caught, lodged, at least as a ghost – but an essential ghost – in every decision, in every event of decision. Its ghostliness deconstructs from within any assurance of presence, any certitude or any supposed criteriology that would assure us of the justice of a decision, in truth of the very event of a decision. (Derrida, 1992: 24–25)

The future is always unpredictable and the arrival of the futures being lived and extrapolated is always potentially near: today's decisions are always tangled up in the undecidability of an open future. Strategic planning is nothing more than a programmable application of imagined calculable and rational events. It is built on the presumption that strategic planning can anticipate future developments. Faced with complex reality, strategic planning trivializes and simplifies it, creating a gap between seemingly clear goals and an open, unpredictable future.

A third, well-known gap is that between planning and implementing. Strategies can only be created according to current problems and the solutions we currently imagine. As long as organizations only have to cope with a trivial world, that's fine. As soon as things become more complex, the simple one-way relation between problem and solution shifts. Solutions for non-trivial problems lead, when isolated from their original context, to a transformation. Regarded from the outside (the preferred manager's view), a strategy may be right; implemented in the organizational context, it turns out to be wrong, because 'actions affect the preferences in the name of which they are taken; and the discovery of new intentions is a common consequence of intentional behaviour' (March, 1981: 176). The plan, therefore, creates a complexity, which cannot be controlled by new plans: following the fatal logic of 'do as before, but more' (Hedberg et al., 1976: 50), the plan merely creates more of the disorder that it had promised to master. Thus, any plan realizes first and foremost the problems of implementation, the process of translation from the strategic vision to the concrete forms. The plan creates with its division of labour between reflecting and implementing the problem it attempts to overcome. It creates the gap that it promised to bridge, constantly, anew.

A fourth gap occurs between planned change and emerging evolution. One can only plan what is already known or in the realm of the imaginable. But as Derrida suggests, the future is always potentially monstrous:

> A future that would not be monstrous would not be a future; it would already be a predictable, calculable, and programmable tomorrow. All experience open to the future is prepared or prepares itself to welcome the monstrous. ... All of history has shown that each time an event has been produced, for example in philosophy or in poetry, it took the form of an unacceptable, or even of the intolerable, of the incomprehensible, that is, of a certain monstrosity. (Derrida, 1995: 386–7)

We might feel disturbed by the strange monsters that threaten our imagination. But monsters cannot be tamed through presentiment: 'One cannot say: "here are our monsters", without immediately turning the monsters into pets' (Derrida, 1990: 80). Similarly, a plan that announces the future immediately turns it into a calculable and linear process. It reduces the monstrous and emergent evolution of the new into a domesticated output. The plan, once a trivial means of achieving ends, turns into a means of trivializing reality.

The fundamental problem is that no one can say in advance whether the moves that an organization makes are useful or not. In fact, future demands may differ from today's insights to such an extent that valuing the category of 'usefulness' might be an error: it is easier to do what is known than what is not, but, as Nietzsche tells, it can be a fatal error:

> Indeed, we have not any organ at all for *knowing*, or for 'truth': we 'know' (or believe, or fancy) just as much as may be *of use* in the interest of the human herd, the species; and even what is here called 'usefulness' is ultimately only a belief, a fancy, and perhaps *the most fatal stupidity by which we shall one day be ruined*. (Nietzsche, 1974: 301, italics added)

Karl Weick (1979) puts it more bluntly as 'Stamp out utility!' Learning and self-organization occurs most readily when what is known in organization theory as slack is encouraged: if there is space for experimentation, foolishness and *randonnée*, where no one calculates every single step, but where one can freely choose between different ways of moving in and of exploring the space. But that is exactly what strategic planning constantly inhibits because it tries to calculate and predict futures instead of allowing its contours to emerge. It creates the gap between goals that are reached successfully, and unfolding opportunities at the margins that are neglected for the simple reason that they are not calculable in advance and thus not a possible subject for the planner's drawing-board or computer screen.

A fifth gap that strategic planning creates is the gap between means and ends. Strategic planning is based on the assumption that it can identify, formulate and communicate one stable common goal that the entire organization should reach. As Luhmann (1973) has shown, goals are neither stable nor is it feasible that one common goal can represent *the* direction towards which the organization is heading. Think of marketing and R&D departments – their individual goals can often be conflicting, contradictory and inconsistent. Thus, the underlying concept that informs strategic planning and that provides its power is basically built on the ignorance of the plurality and contradiction of goals that an organization drives forward. Instead of taking this complexity into account, it creates a gap between seemingly stable ends and apparently rational means; instead of reflecting the interwovenness and mutually constitutive re-creation of means and ends, it divides and thus simplifies their complex interrelation.

Sixth, there is a gap between management planning (head) and the mere inert organization (body). The head leads and the body is expected to follow. Strategy asks for 'strong leaders willing to make choices' (Porter, 1996: 77). It is the general management's core task to formulate strategy:

> The leader must provide the discipline to decide which industry changes and customer needs the company will respond to, while avoiding organizational distractions and maintaining the company's distinctiveness. Managers at lower levels lack the perspective and the confidence to maintain a strategy. ... One of the leader's jobs is to teach others in the organization about strategy – and to say no. (Porter, 1996: 77)

Porter, almost like Taylor a hundred years previously, describes managers as leaders and heroes who think for and teach the organization, confirming the myth of managers as heroic leaders (see Clark and Salaman, 1998). Thus, everyday strategic thinking reinforces the Cartesian split between the intelligible mind and the dumb body that has to be (in)formed. Strategy affects and creates the *identity* of an organization (see Porter, 1996: 77): managers think about a strategy, therefore the organization is. *I think, therefore I am, and they must be.* This linearity leads to unreflexive planning: every plan is a kind of self-description of the organization, to which, to the extent that it sees itself in the image produced and crystallized in the plan, reacts according to the plan; otherwise, it starts to sabotage it. As soon as a plan and its intention are communicated, it starts to change the organization (for instance, some people will support the plan while others start to organize resistance). The simple chain: first management thinks, then organization acts, overlooks feedback, creating complexity that stretches far beyond managerial planning.

Seventh, the plan creates the gap between order and the disorder it supposes to overcome. Strategic planning is a necessity because, otherwise, the organization would drown in its own chaos, thus, the 'strategic agenda demands discipline and continuity; its enemies are distraction and compromise' (Porter, 1996: 78). However, chaos, disorder and noise far from destroying a system, make it more refined.

Fluctuation, disorder, opacity, and noise are not and are no longer affronts to the rational; we no longer speak of this rational, we no longer divvy things up in isms, simple and stiff puzzles, strategic planes for the final conflict. Thus a system has interesting relations according to what is deemed to be its faults or depreciations (Serres, 1982: 13; see Pascale, 1999). Strategic planning that focuses on control and promises to impose an order on organizational activities neglects this complex set of interrelations between order and chaos (see Cooper, 1990; Munro, 2001b). Rather it creates an ordered and cosy realm, as a controllable inside, confronting a more or less chaotic outside, an exterior that constantly threatens its survival. Strategic planning reinforces and deepens this gap: it ignores the complexities and potentialities of 'dis/organization' (Porter, 1996: 78).

In other words, strategy is a complex language game, to use Wittgenstein's (1972) key phrase. It is a language to be mastered and used in order to attain credibility and to appear rational, providing a means of talking about the future while mired in the present. Strategy functions as a language game that holds back doubt, dismay and anxiety. It is a language game for cooling out the fears of senior management, investors, and key stakeholders. It papers over the cracks of present existence and chills out the existential dread that all senior management feel when charged with so much responsibility. It functions as a buffer between individual responsibility and corporate outcomes. Should the future envisioned fail to materialize, then the strategy can be held responsible and the strategy can be changed, and if sacrificial victims are needed to assuage the interests of the various stakeholders, then such strategic sacrifices can be made. Both are possible within the language of strategy.

the language of strategy

Carter and Mueller (2006) argue that in some cases it is very difficult to question a strategy in an organization as it comes to take on a totemic quality (Durkheim, 1975), which imbues it with a sacredness that effectively silences any criticism: to criticize is tantamount to committing heresy. In Enron there was a 'no bad news' policy where it was impossible for staff to air anxieties or question strategy. To question the organization would soon result in an employee being 'ranked and yanked' out of the organization. This is all the more ironic given that Enron's television adverts always emphasized the need to 'ask why' (see Cruver, 2003). Similarly, Judy Bevan's (2002) account of the *Rise and Fall of Marks and Spencer* highlights the way in which, in the 1980s and much of the 1990s, senior management were terrified of questioning the CEO, who was likened to a despotic figure who could brook no dissent or questioning of his decisions.

So is an organization's strategy-making process able to accommodate dissent and subversion? Or is it more readily noteworthy for its totalitarian qualities? As we have seen earlier in this book, talk of resources, capabilities, markets, threats, futures and so forth is very much part of the *lingua franca* of strategy. That is, such terms, and the tools that accompany them, render such subjects knowable and meaningful. They constitute a language game (Wittgenstein, 1972) that is used and reproduced by strategists. It is important to understand how this language game works and what its effects are. Rather than reflecting a reality 'out there', as it were, we are concerned by the way in which such a language game serves to shape and create reality (Clegg et al., 2006). For instance, the creation of strategy in an organization creates new terrain, new possibilities and new realities, an idea informed by constructivist theory (Watzlawick, 1976): far from being out there, waiting patiently to be discovered, 'reality' is the product of our mental constructions. The result of this is that strategic management first delineates a frame within which so-called reality emerges. A SWOT analysis, for instance, divides the world into four realms. With such a matrix in mind, the world comes to be perceived as divided, comprising four fields. Thus, maps create the very territory that they seek to describe (Clegg and Hardy, 1996). Another example would be the way in which an exercise such as scenario planning actively constructs a series of realities (i.e. what does an optimistic scenario looks like? What needs to be achieved in order to achieve it?) The technique therefore creates the very thing it seeks to describe.

The language of strategy provides a map for the future and the ability to construct problems that it then seeks to solve. Strategy, therefore, has the capacity to create problems: it does not simply respond to pre-existing problems. This is a point captured by David Knights and Glenn Morgan (1991: 251), when they note the following: 'In the process of its formulation, strategy is actively involved in the constitution, or re-definition, of problems in advance of offering itself as a solution to them'. The corollary of this is that strategic management maintains and sustains certain problems that are the very *raison d'être* of the organization. Starbuck (1983) has characterized this as an action-generating mode – where new problems are created while appearing to solve old ones.

Of great interest in this context are some of the more practical accounts describing the relationship between language and strategy-making in organizations. For instance, Gordon Shaw, formerly Executive Director of Planning and International at 3M, describes in a fascinating paper the value and the effects of strategic planning through stories (Shaw, 2000; Shaw et al., 1998).

It is the language of strategy that is the defining characteristic of contemporary strategy. It is what delineates strategy in the 'here and now' from what went before. Both Whittington (2000) and Hardy et al. (2000) observe that firms seemed to get on perfectly well without strategic management for much of their history. What they mean is that if one had gone into a medium-sized organization – from either the public or private sector – thirty years ago and asked to see a range of strategy artefacts, such as the mission statement, the vision, the strategic plan, the KPIs, etc., one would probably have been greeted by raised eyebrows and a certain sense of bemusement. The point is that the language game of strategy, as taken for granted by most modern-day strategists, strategy students and organizational actors, is a relatively recent phenomenon. Yet the emergence of the language of strategic management over the last twenty years or so is one of the exemplars of the interchange between large consultancies, business schools, management gurus and organizations. It has provided a common language – a managerial Esperanto perhaps – where managers from different parts of the world, working in different sectors can communicate with each other. Burrell (1996) has referred to such a language as 'MBA speak'. We do not regard this in a pejorative sense but rather as a recognition that the language of strategy has diffused widely throughout the organizational world and that there is an 'emphasis … on the ability to enter strategic "conversations"' (Whittington, 2003: 120) in terms of gaining fluency (cultural capital) in the language of strategy. But there are limits to the aptness of the example of Esperanto. It was, after all, an artificially designed language, filled with a humanist and internationalist vision of humankind, rather than a naturally evolved one. Perhaps the language of strategy is more akin to Basic English – a language used in the 1930s that consisted of 800 or so words which allowed communication but stripped out the ability to express emotion and other human feelings. Basic English was much admired by Stalin and formed the basic of Ingsoc, the language George Orwell devised in his classic dystopian novel *1984* (Orwell, 1949).

So what are the effects of being fluent in the language of strategy? How are we to make sense of why particular strategic tools are used or what particular strategic gambits are in vogue? Quite clearly, the widespread diffusion of particular, highly stylized modes of thinking and representing strategy is illustrative of isomorphism being played out on a grand scale. New institutional theory can tell us much about isopraxism in the strategy field. One of the central contributions of new institutional theory has been to draw attention to the importance that 'legitimacy' plays in organizational life. It has highlighted the way in which organizations behave in order to achieve legitimacy in the eyes of powerful stakeholders (DiMaggio and Powell, 1983/2002). Therefore a university might have a strategic plan in part to appear rational to stakeholders such as government and other funding agencies. Following this line of thinking, strategy discourse has become so pervasive that it is difficult to imagine medium to large organizations without a strategic plan and all the accoutrements – SWOTs, value chains, missions and visions – that go with it. An organization without a panoply of strategic artefacts would, we venture, seem somewhat illegitimate, poorly managed and probably ripe for some sort of takeover.

This conception of strategy has far-reaching implications for the study of strategy. Rather than strategy being able to determine an organization's future, the logic of this position is that the usefulness of strategy rests more in strategy's capacity to provide a means of organizational rationality – an organizational rite. DiMaggio and Powell (1983/2002) identify three forms of isomorphism (regulative, normative and mimetic), all of which have the capacity to tell the story of how highly stylized forms of strategy have been diffused throughout the organizational world. For instance, Carter and Mueller's (2002, 2006) study of CoastElectric, a privatized British utility company, which had for much of its existence had little need for strategic management, found that following privatization the organization's strategists were very clear that the organization 'had' to adopt the accoutrements of strategy. In order to impress stakeholders, strategy had therefore become an obligatory point of passage as a means for producing myths and ceremonies. Meyer and Rowan's (1977) contribution highlights the way in which such an adoption of strategy may play a largely ceremonial role: while strategy will communicate a particular message to key stakeholders, it may well be decoupled from what actually goes on in the organization. But who is doing the decoupling? We may say that strategy is a language game but all such games need players, or actors, who enact the game and play their parts. Who are the strategists?

who are the strategists?

Orthodox strategy has been hugely successful – and so have those whose careers have flourished with it. Strategic managers may well be able to lay claim to impressive credentials and glittering careers, possessing, perhaps, the most elite MBAs. Many students study MBAs with the express intention of becoming a strategist. Indeed, the promotional brochures of many MBA programmes are fairly upfront in the claim that the programme is an ideal preparation for a move into the boardroom – where, according to the popular imagination, strategy gets done. The boardroom meeting marks the state-like cabinet room for strategy – that moment when strategy crystallizes into government. However, all is not well in the world of the MBA. Across Australia and the UK (contexts the authors know well) there has been a significant slackening of demand for the MBA. Given its claims to propel its graduates into top strategy jobs, the diminution of demand seems somewhat counter-intuitive. Perhaps it is because such credentials are valuable 'only to the extent that the future is like the past. In industry after industry, the terrain is changing so fast that experience is becoming irrelevant and even dangerous' (Hamel, 1996: 74).

It may be mistaken to rely on strategy-making that emanates from the inner sanctum, the gilded elite, or the generals, of an organization. All elite's tend towards ossification, as elite theory since Pareto (1968) and Mosca (1939) has taught us, and become vulnerable to the veritable seductions of their own power and strategies. That is, they find themselves unable to do little else other than reproduce what worked for them, or the organization, at a different time and in a different space. Fighting the last war is how the military describe it. Fighting against it requires what some strategists – well, at least Mao Tse-Tung and Tom Peters – refer to as 'Cultural Revolution'. Mao tried it and it was a disaster; Peters advocates it normatively but we are unaware of whether, if it has been enacted, it has been successful. We doubt it: the hypothesis of the circulation of elites is well founded: changing the culture of the cadres by creating a state of permanent revolution tends to lead to confusions in identity, practice and career. Strategy-making requires a circulatory elite; it requires new blood defined by new ideas, which, if the ideas do not work, can make way for the new elite. Strategy should be an open, inclusive process.

While much is known about those who occupy professional (Abbott, 1988) or knowledge-worker (Alvesson, 1993, 2001) positions within organizations, and the consultants (Clark and Fincham, 2002) who advise them, comparatively little is known about strategists. Given that they occupy undoubtedly powerful positions that can have far-reaching effects on society, this is problematic. Future research will hopefully provide us with more of a sense of 'who become strategists?' and 'what are their collective biographies?' At the moment, we would speculate that very often strategists in positions of power are disproportionately drawn from the gilded elite of upper middle-class, middle-aged, white males? So in anthropological parlance, who is *homo strategicus*? And how do they maintain their dominance? What are their strategies for maintaining their strategic position within their organizations? How do they retain their grip on power? Thus, it would be interesting to know how strategists are constructed and what material makes them up? How does a strategist actually become a strategist? What rites of passage do they experience in their move from the realm of operational activities to the rarefied heights of strategy-making? Does it involve a secondment to a project team, followed by a move to head office? Each large organization is likely to have its own pathway through which people become strategists. In some cases, this might be fairly easy for newcomers to the organization to work out, while in other, more Byzantine places, it might be altogether more mysterious.

With most professions and many occupational groups, it is pretty clear what education and training they have received to carry out their role. But this is far from clear with strategists. Questions are: What prepared them for their role as strategists? How did they acquire their strategic cultural capital? Mindful of the huge expansion of MBA education over the last two decades, do strategists learn their strategy as part of an MBA syllabus? And, if so, how do they practise evidence-based strategy when their basic knowledge resources may already be one or two generations old? We know that the best practitioner-oriented journals, such as the *Harvard Business Review*, seek to bridge the education gap, but how successful are they? With what frequency do which types of strategist read what sources of information and participate in what seminar? Our colleague, Alan McKinlay (2002), carried out a study in a large pharmaceutical company and one of his chief findings was that all aspirant strategists in the organization read *The Economist* magazine voraciously. In their meetings with senior management, those who had retained the arguments from *The Economist* were then able to cast themselves as erudite, well-educated cosmopolitans – just the right sort of material for doing serious strategy! But be warned, in other contexts, such as seminars about strategy, merely parroting *The Economist* could have very different effects!

There is a serious issue generally within professional education relating to the link between the canons of knowledge available, the sites in which they are disseminated and learned and the changes that these canons undergo in application. What do strategists actually do when doing strategy? Does an experienced strategist, for example, actively draw on the Porter they picked up in a course, or do they reach for the nostrums gleaned from Mintzberg? Or if a strategist does use ideas they picked up at business school, is this a conscious process, or have the ideas become second nature? Theses issues link in with a discussion around the education of medics and teachers (Abbott, 1988). The question is the extent to which formally encoded and learnt knowledge can be considered to be arcane or perfomative. Andrew Abbott's point is: what formal knowledge studied by doctors or teachers is actually used in their practice? To what extent is such an education process to be seen as being, in part, a rite of passage? Translated into our discussion, one argument would be that the strategy knowledge gained on a strategy course has very little to do with any subsequent practice as a strategist, that it is a rite of passage whereby the aim is to pass the exam and, once that hurdle is negotiated, the knowledge ceases to be relevant. An alternative view would be that the education received on a strategy course is an essential prerequisite to being a strategist. So does the 'case method' approach of MBAs, taken together with the content of strategy courses, prepare MBA students for a life of 'doing strategy'?

What do we know of the identities of strategists? Power can be a productive force, as Michel Foucault (1977) perceptively noted. What do we know of how strategists view themselves? What is their self-image? Do they, for instance, construct their subjectivities through the exciting discourse of strategy? Are they the happening poster boys and girls of the new economy? Or, perhaps the stressed-out, time-poor executives dreaming of downshifting to a slower pace of life? Or maybe Quixote-like characters dreaming of struggles and victories yet to happen? How is the identity of the strategist formed when they live in a here and now that requires them to make it a tomorrow that may never come? What does it mean to be condemned to live in the potentially future imperfect of their prognoses?

It is clearly important to have a sense of who the strategists are, yet we should sound a note of caution about concentrating overly on the agency of successful strategists – a course of action that runs the danger of lapsing into an atavistic account of heroic tales from the boardroom and regarding failure as something from which either no lessons can be learnt or as something to be ignored. Additionally, there is the risk, either way, of over-dramatizing the role of the individual. Although it has only been a characteristic of narrative styles for the last three centuries, stories that focus on the dramatic orchestrations of human agency are by now utterly dominant. It used to be the gods who determined the fate of men and women; now, at least in MBAs, it is the strategists. What about the role of impersonal agencies (Clegg, 1989)? The mechanical failure that grounded the aeroplane bearing the player whose advice would have made all the difference, the virus that ate the strategy on the strategist's computer, or the market meltdown which blew everything out of the water? A means of guarding against such a tendency is by recognizing the existence of non-human actors that can play an important role in the making of strategy. Donald MacKenzie's (2006) fascinating analyses of financial instruments and how they create markets are a good example of this. In looking at the 1987 stock market crash in the United States – the gravest financial crisis America had faced since the Wall Street Crash – MacKenzie highlights the way in which a fairly routine technical practice brought the stock market to its knees. Blackler et al.'s research (2000) highlighted the pivotal role of whiteboards in the innovation process (see Eden and Ackerman, 1998). It was a whiteboard – or rather what was not recorded as being on it – which served as one of the occasions that the opposition was able to exploit to help the federal government in Australia lose the 1996 election. What was in question was the ethics of a political party that dispensed money as electoral bribes to those constituencies that voted for it. In an odd quirk of politics, the government that was elected was to lose office three elections later in 2007 with similar ethical issues being raised against it – that its expenditures were political bribes systematically skewed towards its key electorates. In the interim, the corporate world globally was rocked by a series of ethical scandals, of which Enron was the most widely reported. Ethics and strategy were recoupled on the agenda.

A hallmark of traditional liberal professions is the existence of a governing body and a code of conduct for its practitioners. While recent events in the form of accounting and medical scandals serve as a reminder that such codes may be somewhat decoupled from the praxis of everyday professional life, nonetheless, it is noteworthy that, in comparison, contemporary notions of strategic thought remain remarkably silent on the issue of ethics. What are the ethics that are to underpin strategy? For instance, Enron was one of the prime recruiters of MBA graduates from elite North American business schools. The organization fostered a competitive environment which encouraged strategists to cut corners and take risks. Brian Cruver was one such MBA graduate recruited to Enron, and his book, published after the collapse of Enron, is a sobering story of hubris and greed (Cruver, 2003). Equally, McClean and Elkind's *The Smartest Guys in the Room* (2006) is a damning indictment of the corruption and aggressive behaviour that underpinned the Enron story – a story once lavished with praise by Gary Hamel (1996). How are we to make sense of the role that business schools have played in this? Have they inculcated their students with the sense of 'anything goes' and 'win at all costs', while clearing up the resultant mess is someone else's problem? If this is the case, what are the implications for organizations and society of the coming of age of the 'business school' generation?

strategy and ethics

Efforts to conceptualize war were the soil in which strategy was first nurtured and cultivated. Strategy was, from its very beginnings, linked to war. As the Prussian military theorist Carl von Clausewitz (1968:

165) advised in his book *On War*, published 1832, strategy 'forms the plan of the war, and to this end it links together the series of acts which are to lead to the final decision, that is to say, it makes the plans for the separate campaigns and regulates the combats to be fought in each'. Reading Mintzberg one and a half centuries later, the link between the martial beginnings and organizational adaptation of the concept of strategy becomes evident. Recall that for Mintzberg, strategic positioning could be understood as 'consisting of a *launching* device, representing an organization, that send *projectiles*, namely products and services, at a landscape of *targets*, meaning markets, faced with *rivals*, or competition, in the hope of attaining *fit*' (Mintzberg, 1998: 93, emphasis added). Obviously phallocentric, this thinking is inspired by war metaphors in which the organization is a mere vehicle of the managerial war machinery (see Ross-Smith and Kornberger, 2004).

In the past, war was supposed to be a chivalrous as well as a bloody affair, though if this ever was the case, the twentieth century surely destroyed such an illusion. It was held to possess a certain code of ethics, but what of its bastard offspring strategy? Deducing clues from this relationship between strategy and war, it is hardly surprising that strategy and ethics make for something of an odd couple. Whereas ethics might scrutinize the value of an 'end', strategy focuses on the right use of 'means' to achieve the strategically most favourable 'end' – regardless of its ethical implications. It is, perhaps, not surprising, that strategy is not necessarily a highly ethical enterprise. Where there are many competitors and only one winner, and where the rewards for victory are so high, would one expect it be otherwise?

Strategy-making is necessarily an activity in which the social practice of ethics is at stake. All games are, by definition, ethical. They entail notions of correct or fair play as well as winners and losers. The winners have lots of advantages of incumbency, of being in that position. How winners get to defeat and create losers can, at least for a while, be seen as the basis for a winning strategy, irrespective of the costs. There is a sense in which strategy, as a language game, provides us with the heroes and villains of the contemporary corporate world. Indeed, as the case of characters, such as the late Kenneth Lay, the CEO of Enron, suggest, the roles may often be filled at different times by the same actor. Strategy writes scripts for adulation today which can as easily be rescripted as shaming and deceitful tomorrow. Strategy is a strange game in one respect, however: there is no referee or umpire policing every stage of the game play, and the adulation of the crowd – expressed through the markets – provides the basis for a morality of judgement based on good plays. The favours of the market can be a fickle and decisive ethical task-master, however. The very thing that makes a company rich, powerful and successful, can make the same organization poor, its executive's criminals, and its investor's debtors, as we have seen with countless corporate scandals. It is easy to get caught up in the success of a winning strategy and be blind to the corners it cuts. Winning is its own justification, but it is no guarantee of continued success or legitimacy, although it may make it more likely.

Strategy displays symbolic manifestations that seek to frame and shape the dominant order of the organization, generating a system of highly visible distinctions and discriminations which stratify the availability and appropriateness of the privileged discourses. Such a symbolic order is never stable or fixed but always an effect of previous and current power relations and competitions in which actors seek to define their strategy. Hence the analysis of the symbols, artefacts and language of strategy would be critical to understanding strategy as practice.

Sometimes that which is left unsaid is more important than that which is carefully articulated. The silences of strategy, from the words it doesn't pronounce, speak as much as those it does. The silences and gaps in a discourse are significant to its understanding. These indicate the unconscious of the discourse, in so far as it possesses one, an unconscious in which the play of history beyond its edges may be seen. The unconsciousness of the discourse of strategy as practice constitutes the silences of everyday organizational life: the non-issues, non-decision-making, the exclusions from the agenda, the overlooked and unnoted actors, acts and omissions, those things that are strategically unthinkable, telling the truth about the pollution 'externalities' of present practices rather than lobbying for looser regulation, being honest about the health risks to children and young people who eat food products that are heavily promoted and heavily saturated with trans-fats, or admitting that the dream machine of the moment is a heavily expensive, gas-guzzling SUV with an unstable centre of gravity, a greater propensity to kill pedestrians who get in its way, and which does greater damage to smaller vehicles.

Strategy relations display symbolic manifestations that order the dominant symbols of the organization, generating a system of highly visible distinctions and discriminations which stratify the availability and appropriateness of the available discourses. Such a symbolic order is never stable or fixed but an effect of previous and current power relations and competitions in which actors seek to define their strategy. Knowledge is always contested and reality is something known only through knowledge of it – hence, as Žižek (2005: 271) says, 'there is no transcendental Signified; so-called reality is a discursive construct; every given identity, including that of a subject is an effect of contingent differential relations'. Strategies are an effect of the play of contingent discursive possibilities, the signification of which is not fixed in advance because all of its possible terms are relational. It is the play of differences that is important.

Strategy is always a work in process. The indetermination of strategies, however, is a piece of social construction that takes place in an already structured space of significations, privileges and practices. Not only officially formulated strategists have strategies. Strategy is more properly conceived as a discourse in which some voices may not be attended to for some time, but which can, if insistent and well-organized, make it on to the agenda. The best example of this is the way that the ecological critique of global warming now shapes many major corporations' strategies. Our point is that what is formulated as strategy in official, formal terms needs to be seen, analytically, by researchers in terms of the possible range of strategies – both those that emanate from official formulations and those that derive from unofficial glosses on these formulations as signs of what might be but is not. The distinction between 'formulation' and 'gloss', of course, derives from what we have argued is the real progenitor of a practice-based approach – the ethnomethodology of Garfinkel (1967). Especially useful here will be those stakeholders who deliberately take an oppositional stance to existing strategy: the eco-warriors, the NGOs, and so on. It is from these stakeholders that strategic innovations will emerge. Analyzing strategy is not merely reporting what it is that is done, but also what is not done in terms of the constitution of issues for the agenda. To not do this is merely to report what strategy is, rather than analyze how its distinctiveness is defined in a world of possibilities. Thus, strategy conceived in research terms, as practices that focus solely on that which strategists said and did, will miss the strategic spaces within which strategy is constituted. What is necessary is to explore not only what is done but what is not done, that which is not practised, that which is not said, using external stakeholder articulations.

conclusion

Researchers should capture the strategic contra-suggestions of activist stakeholders and expose them to the official strategists, record their responses in order to capture the official line, and then feed them back to the dissident stakeholders for further comment. In this way, the silences, the non-issues, the non-decisions and the non-agendas can be raised to a matter of practice. Hatch and Schultz (2002) suggest a highly dynamic process, linking the organization's strategy (official images), as it is socially constructed by strategists and the top-management team, with images of that strategy constructed by others (stakeholders' images). Their model seeks to represent the complexity of these processes, in terms of the numerous interactions that transpire, as more parties are brought into the organizational strategy conversation in the interrogative and continuous process that the researcher makes. An interplay is set up between the official voices of the organization and its stakeholders, which can become as interactive as the researcher wishes to make it. Research traces the path by which emergent understandings and expressions of the organization's strategy and its meaning(s) and multiple interpretations are constructed and engaged by different communities of practice interested in the strategy process. The researcher becomes an aide to polyphony and the creative – and sometimes acrimonious – conversations that can ensue, while piling up deeply layered and Geertzian (1973) 'thick' descriptions of the strategy process, its exclusions and inclusions.

9

In Conclusion …
the Futures of Strategy?

▬▬▬ introduction

This book has aimed to be a critical introduction to strategy. In the last eight chapters we have toured strategy. We have strolled down its brightly lit boulevards, taken short-cuts through back alleys, and occasionally ventured into the sleazy side of town, for example, the price-fixers exploiting their customers. Very often we have been critical of many of the best-known theories in strategy, while we have identified other ideas, particularly from organization theory, philosophy and sociology, as being useful resources for better strategy. In our journey into strategy's interior, we have taken a deeply political view of the field. We see strategy as an inextricably political activity that takes place in a highly politicized world. For those looking for practical manuals on how to do strategy, we would encourage you to walk past the shelves stuffed with 'how to do it' guides by wannabe management gurus and instead head for books on power, Machiavelli's *The Prince* being the fountainhead.

From a Machiavellian perspective, understanding strategy necessitates an engagement with power and politics. This would involve looking at what decisions are made (and why), how non-decision-making takes place (i.e. through keeping items off the agenda), as well as the means through which dominant elites successfully exercise hegemonic control over strategy-making. Alastair Campbell's diaries (2007) of his tenure as Tony Blair's spin doctor provide a fascinating account of the way in which decisions are made and also issues, such as the UK joining the euro, are kept off the agenda. Campbell's diaries also point to the power of external interests such as media moguls – often citizens of countries far away from the UK – in dictating 'acceptable' policy. Those interested in strategy would do well to look back at released government records to see the micro-detail of how decisions were made and the power plays that were pivotal to their making. The legendary rivalry between Tony Blair – Campbell's boss – and Gordon Brown – Blair's successor – is not discussed in any great depth, which is an example of a 'non-issue' being created.

Our views on strategy are interested in what voices are heard when strategy is being formulated. What implications do those voices heard and those silenced have for the strategy-making process? A frequently cited example of this is the Kennedy government's decision to invade Cuba, which resulted in the Bay of Pigs disaster. The post-mortem conducted by the Kennedy government following the débâcle highlighted the problem of groupthink – a small cabal of like-minded people reaching the same conclusions. It was a clear demonstration that if the formulation of strategy is restricted to the comfy confines of the corporate elite, often they will reach very poor decisions. Fifty years after Kennedy's government learnt this to their cost, one could be mistaken for thinking that very few strategists have taken this lesson on board. Think of Iraq, for instance. The problem is that confining strategy-making to elites often ends up merely reproducing the prejudices and biases of that managerial elite. To understand power, therefore, is to go to the heart of key questions: What is deemed admissible within a strategy-making environment and by whom is it admissible? Is the organization suitably democratic, such that it discovers and utilizes what James March (1971) described as the 'technology of foolishness', where people from the boundaries of an organization – young people, newcomers, minorities (put simply, people with different perspectives) – are able to contribute to the strategy-making process? As strategists know, people from the periphery – Simmelian 'strangers' (Simmel, 1950) such as newcomers and outsiders – often think more creatively because they are 'exposed to ideas and developments that do not conform to the company's orthodoxies' (Hamel, 1996: 77). They have not become so practised in the arts of deception that constitute dominant accounts of strategy that they are unable to think creatively.

opening up strategy

The historian Paul Veyne has developed a particularly useful concept of practice that can be applied to a power-full conception of strategy. In Veyne's view (1997: 153), practice 'is not some mysterious agency, some substratum of history, some hidden engine; it is what people do (the word says just what it means)'. He implies that we should not judge people according to their ideologies. It is deeds rather than words that matter most when the two diverge. We should not assume that terms such as strategy denote some essential activity, always the same, everywhere. Rather, Veyne suggests that such seemingly objective terms as strategy can only ever be the correlate of specific practices. Following this perspective, strategy as an object of analysis is explained by what went into its making, and not the other way round (that the object that is taken to be strategy explains how it is made up). The strategy we assume we observe is a result of an assemblage of practices. It is only the process of objectifying and reifying these practices that leads to what we think of as objects.

Think of strategy as an example: we know that some companies do well without it, that some strategies emerge, while others are implemented top-down. The object 'strategy' does not exist as starting point: only the practices associated with the word makes us believe that strategy is a 'thing' that can be observed, crafted and managed in departments, whereas it is, in fact, only a projection of possible practices – practices that might differ and change fundamentally from one setting of strategy to another. The problem is if one starts with the object 'strategy' and tries to explain how it got manufactured; rather, we should forget (for a moment, at least) the word 'strategy' and see which practices produce endurable or recurring events that eventually turn into 'things' or 'events' that are then addressed as 'strategy'.

Hence, we have good reason to assume that strategy does not exist independently of a set of practices that form its base. In fact, strategy might happen in different departments, in different circumstances and different contexts. However, only a small percentage of actions that occur will be called 'strategic' because they revolve around a set of practices that constitute what is formally acknowledged to be strategy. From this perspective, our interest in looking at strategy from the vantage point of power and politics would involve researching those practices that constitute the object of 'strategy'. Key questions would include: Which routines make an action or an event strategic? For instance, when and why does an informal gathering become labelled strategic? When does a report become a visionary and strategic document? What artefacts and symbols are involved in the creation and legitimization of those strategic objects? For instance, while a strategy may be deemed to be created when a strategic plan has been produced and then approved at a Board of Directors meeting, maybe it is rather more the case that the strategy is legitimized by a ritualized event, such as a Board meeting? Or does strategy rely on some sort of external actor approving it, such as a powerful media mogul in the case of politics or, in the case of many strategies that are designed to limit competition, such as price-fixing agreements where it may well be competitors that approve it? Which performative language games are deployed in the creation of strategy? And, most importantly, what is excluded from the agenda of strategy-makers? What are the issues that strategists consciously keep off the strategy agenda because they know that they would be unacceptable to the powers that be? Such an approach would not assume that given subjects, called 'strategists', were necessarily the authors of strategy. Rather, it is the practices and rituals of strategy-making that might constitute a person as a strategist. Mastering a certain language, tools and habitus might allow people to position themselves as having the status of 'a strategist' ascribed to them. Hence a practice approach might help us to understand what constitutes a strategist as a subject (and not assume top management to be strategists a priori).

These questions open up the field of strategy research: strategy only exists as an object constituted by a certain practice. However, the practice itself is not a priori or beforehand strategic in any respect (Veyne, 1997: 167). Only after the fact, for instance, can we recognize the strategic folly of Easter Islanders in allowing their island to be denuded of trees, either through their agency or that of the rats that they inadvertently introduced to the island (there is some dispute as to whose agency it was) or of medieval Norse folk insisting on grazing cows in a habitat, Greenland, that was unsuited to them (Diamond, 1998). These practices were strategic – they caused each society to collapse – but were not regarded so at the time because the practices which inscribed these actions were deeply, culturally mundane.

In this respect, writers such as Machiavelli could be read as anthropologies of power conceived as strategy (e.g. Clegg, 1989). From the power perspective, one would focus on how coalitions are formed and on how people holding positions of power are enrolled so that they support a given strategy. The failure of the attempt by the United States government to get a United Nations resolution sanctioning an invasion of Iraq provides a *Realpolitik* insight into how creating coalitions can be difficult. The power perspective on strategy would also seek to explore the control of obligatory points of passage and their role in the strategy-making process. For instance, the sources of advice that are not sought may be as important as those that are, especially in a corporate context where the top-management team may be less than a balance of all the disciplines, skewed, perhaps, to just one or two disciplines, such as Finance or Production, such that the views of HRM and Marketing hardly enter into consideration. Strategy from a power perspective would also concentrate on capturing of the right rhetorical tone, the building of convincing discursive scenarios, and so on. From this perspective the apparent rationality behind strategy can be seen as an instrument used to create legitimacy that uses rationality as a façade and ceremony (Meyer and Rowan, 1977), offering organized space for hypocrisy (Brunsson, 1985). Many governments, for example, are only too keen to privatize certain parts of their asset portfolio, such as the airports or airlines, because they no longer have to take the flack about issues such as the noise generated by airport usage. Shifting the asset to private hands means that the responsibility for the consequences of the activity associated with the asset no longer flows through state channels: the obligatory passage points have been re-routed.

In our view, strategy is indistinguishable from the accounts of it that its actors generate. The practice of strategy would be akin to Flyvbjerg's (2001) account of the way that authorities rationalize particular versions of their rationality as what must be done – in the name of strategy. Bearing the name of strategy, a particular form of rationality gets made up; one that is very good at rationalizing and sanctioning itself in the name of the 'bigger picture', the 'mission', 'the future', and other heroic images. Overwhelmingly, strategy projects itself politically through inter-organizational power relations.

strategy as inter-organizational power relations

Power relates to strategy not only through relations within the organization, but also through relations outside. Just as strategists need to consider how the organization will achieve its goals *vis-à-vis* markets, competitors and customers, they must also think about strategic power globally. When corporations are multinational, they will become players in international relations, usually thought of as the preserve of states. As we saw earlier in the book, strategy does not deal at all well with the state. It lacks a theory of the state, which seriously limits its capacity to make sense of what is going on in the geopolitical sphere. State theory is a branch of sociology and political science which does make sense of the geopolitical in ways that the economic rationalism of strategies' primary roots do not (see van Creveld, 1999). Of course, as van Creveld suggests, for much of what used to be the exclusive sphere of state activity, it is no longer the case that the state rules unequivocally. The most fundamental state action is the pursuit of war, using the legitimate monopoly of the means of violence that the state enjoys to do so. However, as the extensive outsourcing of much of the supply chain for the Second Gulf War on Iraq and the role of private enterprise in the subsequent occupation of that country shows, it is corporations as well as states that engage in warfare and international relations today. Where companies such as Blackstone and Haliburton have a major role to play in post-war occupation and 'reconstruction', then they have to have some strategic understanding of international relations.

As Sven Behrendt (2007) has argued, multinational strategists have to operate in and understand various political systems. At the core of these systems are the power relations of various national governments. The interests that multinational strategists have to advance often mean that they cannot owe loyalty to their national governments as they seek to advance company value. Moreover, they will be working internationally in territories with governments of many different hues. How they interpret and make sense of these governments and their state strategies will be vital to the success of corporate strategy.

Writers of strategy texts, typically, seem to assume that strategists operate with pro-business and anti-government ideologies, given the scantiness of their consideration of state action in other than stereotypical terms. Porter (1990) is a good example. For instance, in his account of the competitive strategies of nations there is little serious consideration given to the state in anything other than a neo-liberal caricature. Interestingly, the Porter brand became so influential around the world that many governments sought strenuously to limit their capabilities so that they accorded with Porter's caricature of them, often as a result of tutelage from the central Finance Ministries (Pusey, 1991).

Ideally, strategy texts assume that the strategists can operate with total power, that their desire for unrestricted access to resources and markets throughout the world should be achievable, and that they should have the freedom to integrate core activities with other operations across national boundaries. To do this they would need to coordinate and control all aspects of a company on a worldwide basis. On this basis, they can maximize shareholder value and minimize taxes. To minimize taxes they will often seek to establish corporate headquarters in low tax regimes such as Dutch Antilles or the Cayman Islands. Light regulatory frameworks and minimal government expenditures are desirable in home territory so that less tax is required. Corporations have a bottom line to which they can reduce costs and benefits unambiguously and can afford to think of global competitiveness globally. What are desirable from their point of view are minimal government regulation and taxation, plus a reasonable propensity for governments to offer grants and subsidies for local investment. Often, they will expect governments to cover the costs of basic infrastructure, such as the funding of basic and high-risk research, universities and vocational training systems, the promotion and funding of the dissemination of scientific and technical information and technology transfer, as well as economic and physical security and a communications infrastructure, such as high-speed broadband links. Tax incentives will be sought for investment in industrial R&D and technological innovations as well as guarantees that national enterprises have a stable home base. Privileged access to the domestic market will be expected via public contracts (defence, telecommunications, health, transport, education and social services). Appropriate industrial policies will be sought, particularly for those in the high-technology strategic sectors (defence, telecommunications and data processing). Strategists will be keen to stress the mobility and logic of capital as profit and economic rent-seeking. If the local state does not provide the required sweeteners, then they will be keen to maintain the narrative that mobile capitalism will simply exit the scene and set up where the benefits sought can be ensured. The rationalities of government and commerce differ greatly. Neither home base nor host country governments necessarily share interests with the transnational organizations that straddle them. It might be remarked, in a Machiavellian vein, that in business there are no allies, only interests.

In terms of host countries, strategists have to adapt their companies to the preferences of governments, regulators and global policymakers where they operate. Governments want many different things, depending on the type of state in which they operate. In democratic states they want to be re-elected. While it is electors that re-elect them, rather than corporations, corporation strategists can stress issues on which their interests align with voters: electors are presumed to enjoy low taxes and so do corporations. However, voters also want extensive social programmes for health, education and retirement. Clever corporation strategists will work assiduously in the media, in lobbying and in developing strategies to suggest that these can only really be afforded through private insurance-based and supplied programmes, the alternative being excessive taxation and 'socialist' programmes.

Business strategists need to understand the state, an argument that we have made earlier in the book, as something other than the liberal specification of business ideologies. Although the liberal frame is the dominant way of viewing business–state relations, as Behrendt (2007) argues, the frame of understanding with which strategists approach the vexed question of business–state relations makes a considerable difference. While liberalism may be a favoured frame, it is neither the only nor the most sophisticated way of grasping the external world in which strategy operates. Drawing on the international relations literature, he notes that there are five views of the structure of the global political environment:

- Hegemony
- New Realism
- Institutionalism
- Liberalism, and
- Postmodern Anarchy.

While each of these perspectives is coherent, each suggests a different strategic approach to international expansion, and each fits best with a different set of companies. We shall briefly review each of these.

Hegemony: dominant states.   At the close of the twentieth century this was the dominant strategic lens. From this perspective, international stability oscillates around a hegemonically powerful state that articulates and enforces the rules of power relations globally. After the demise of the Soviet system, this appeared to be the future with the USA cast as the global hegemon – an age of a New Empire steered by a US economy made vigorous through technological and economic leadership and military strength. Historically, of course, this strength was based on an almost permanent war footing and its associated military-industrial complex. Just counting the major wars that the USA has been involved in during the last fifty years or so, there have been remarkably few periods when the USA has not been at war:

- Second World War: three years, eight months in the Pacific (December 1941 to August 1945)
- Formal peace (1945–50)
- Korean War: three years, one month (June 1950 to July 1953)
- Formal peace (1953–64) – Much covert and overt involvement in various Latin American coups, counter-insurgencies and military dictatorships
- Vietnam War: eight years, five months (August 1964 to January 1973).
- Formal peace (1973–1991) – Much covert involvement in Middle Eastern instability and overt and covert involvement in various Latin American coups, counter-insurgencies and military dictatorships
- Persian Gulf War: one and a half months (January to February in 1991)
- Formal peace (1991–2001) – Involvement in various East African campaigns, such as Sudan
- Afghanistan: over six years (since October 2001)
- Iraq: over five years (since March 2003)

In fact, 'America is a country that is comfortable with war. In the 230 years since the Declaration of Independence, the US has invaded other countries on more than 200 occasions, according to the Congressional Research Service. That is an average of one foreign incursion every 14 months in the nation's history' (Hartcher, 2008). Undoubtedly, war has been good for business: it has acted as a major spur for innovation, investment, product development and trials, and destruction of capital stock and infrastructure, generating renewed investment opportunities. Of course, a few people get damaged in this war-enhanced circulation of capital – but that's business. In fact, war is such a good thing for business that it becomes generalized into a process that does not even require *specific* antagonists. For instance, it becomes a war on abstract nouns, such as 'terror', a signifier that seems to float on a sea of oil and fundamentalism – on all sides.

At the close of the Cold War, the USA was undoubtedly a global hegemon. Behrendt (2007) suggests that a corporate strategy informed by hegemonic stability theory follows the lead of the hegemonic nation. Strategy follows the flag. A substantial part of business operations will be contained within either the consumer market of the dominant state or within those markets that it dominates hegemonically. The hegemonic state protects business within its sphere of influence through diverse regulatory and structural policies. The military-industrial complex presents huge opportunities for investment and R&D. The symbols and images that the hegemon displays around the world presents great opportunities for a free ride in marketing terms, and military leadership models and business models will borrow heavily from each other – the emblematic figure of Robert McNamara comes to mind. Management style will be highly centralized, authoritarian by instinct, and deeply unreflexive towards expressions of political, cultural and ideological difference. Many American corporations benefited in the post-war era from US hegemony, with Coca-Cola being the most obvious.

New Realism: balance of power.   In this view, corporations operate in a global system of states. These states are engaged in a constant relational struggle. While such power relations might seem to be inherently unstable, most of the time the situation is stable. There is a balance of power. The classic example of this was the situation for most of the latter half of the twentieth century, when the world was divided into two rival blocs under Soviet and US hegemony, respectively. After the Cold War ended, the situation became more complicated: there is one hegemon whose power appears to be in relative decline – the USA – and many regional hegemons, such as the European Union, China and Russia, countries such as Iran, North Korea and Venezuela, which challenge regional hegemony, and emergent sub-hegemons, such as Brazil and India.

As Behrendt (2007) argues, New Realism suggests that, strategically, corporations will seek self-sufficiency within various power centres. For instance, rather than exposing the corporation to the instabilities of power relations between hegemonic blocs, the strategy will be to try to ensure stability within the hegemonic bloc. An example would be developing supply chains within regional commercial centres rather than going to the cheapest provider if they are outside the bloc. Behrendt suggests that management structures will be decentralized, with a global headquarters providing limited corporate functions and mediating the interests of business units operating in different global regions. Corporations should reflect the regional characteristics of the hubs in which they operate and have some commitment to formal diversity strategies, while marketing strategies will cater to distinctively differentiated cultural markets rather than worldwide brands. Behrendt suggests that the oil industry typically operates from a New Realism world view, navigating the nationalist objectives of governments around the globe, such as Medvedev's Russian government, with its aggressive re-nationalization of their oil industry, or Chavez's Venezuelan strategy of re-nationalization.

Institutionalism: global rules.   Institutionalists favour negotiated order in international affairs with good governance and strong rules. Thus, ideally, the world would be governed effectively by a global institutional framework in which the United Nations manages peace and war, the World Trade Organization should enforce rules of free trade, the Kyoto Protocol regulates responses to global warming, the World Bank encourages global economic development, the International Monetary Fund promotes sound economies, and the Organization for Economic Cooperation and Development will promote good national governance. Multilateral trade arrangements, the international protection of intellectual property rights, and standardization of labour and environmental regulations characterize the institutionalist view of the world, as Behrendt (2007) suggests. Transnational corporations would be free to roam globally in this view: global supply chains could snake everywhere and standardized products would be distributed throughout the world. As a perspective, it combines elements of classical liberalism and free trade together with a realization that only strong global institutions can shape a world which is free for trade. Pharmaceutical, bioscience and high-tech industries dependent on consistent innovation and rigorous intellectual property rights, tend to view the world through the lens of institutionalism, Behrendt suggests. They participate in shaping and championing international rules. Typically, they have management structures based on a strong central administration and command structures.

Liberalism: social order.   Classical liberal thought in international relations was sketched by nineteenth-century theorists such as Herbert Spencer, who foresaw that trade would replace war as the major mechanism for adjusting power relations between states. Liberalism assumes that complex transnational interdependencies are driven by decreasing transaction costs, while war and violence become less important, thus the chances for cooperation among states increase. Also, in contemporary times, such cooperation will be supported by increasingly powerful societal actors such as non-governmental organizations – think of Greenpeace or Oxfam. Corporations that are strategically fit for liberalism would be loose-knit 'movements', Behrendt suggests, usually with flat management structures in which managers act as visionaries, setting the principles but letting colleagues negotiate the details. Diversity will be essential: in the workforce, culture, gender, and socially. Diversity will enable more strategic responses to the heterogeneity encountered in a global liberal order. In a liberal world market those products that can appeal across the intersectional lines of difference that distinguish people will be most effective. McDonald's is a classic example, as the American sociologist George Ritzer (2004) recognized when he coined the term 'McDonaldization'. It refers to the application of technical rationality to all areas of human life. It is, as Ritzer acknowledges, a contemporary variant on the Weberian theme of the rationalization of the world.

Postmodern Anarchy: fatalism.   When the strategist looks at the world as a whole, not everywhere represents a liberal marketplace. Some places have insufficient effective demand. For instance, outside corrupt oligarchs and despots, much of Africa can be written out of the picture, except for purposes of resource extraction. Especially, those parts of the globe subject to resurgent and fundamentalist Islam, such as Iraq and Afghanistan, offer little opportunity to the liberal strategist. The nation-state cannot secure order in these benighted world regions. Where governments fail the Hobbesian task of establishing sovereignty Behrendt (2007) sees commercial opportunities for what he terms the anarchic corporation that exploits markets wherever possible, converting huge transaction costs and collateral damages into commercial activities – think of Haliburton, Blackstone and the Australian Wheat Board in Iraq, where the major relational devices used strategically become guns and bribes. Short-term market share is what counts; hearts and minds, brand loyalty and identification are unimportant because long-lasting customer loyalty is unlikely. Regimes change rapidly, local gangsterism often rules rather than national government and deals will tend to be highly local, unstable and contingent on *ad hoc* relations.

▨▨▨▨ conclusion

Corporate strategy has to engage in practice with a political environment. The world in which they operate is political and companies need to recognize that political analysis is an essential piece of the global strategy toolkit. Corporations shape the evolution of the global world and, just as states must develop strategies for international relations, so must corporations. And corporations and states are increasingly intertwined. In part, this is a result of the downsizing of the scope of state activities, as neo-liberal economic agendas have seen the state withdraw in many countries from many activities, such as telecommunications, airlines, energy utilities, and such like. Other services that were once almost wholly state-provided to citizens, such as health or education, in many countries are increasingly offered to customers on the market. Many things that states once did almost in their entirety, such as wage war, are increasingly contracted out. In the second Gulf War fought in Iraq, many essential supply and service functions, as well as security functions for the occupying powers, were provided by the private sector. One consequence is that the strategies of companies such as Haliburton or Blackstone increasingly become tied up with the strategies of states such as the USA. It seems evident that, in future, corporate strategists will need to take international strategy more seriously. Moreover, international strategists will need to start waking up to the powerful role of corporations in the field of global strategy and realize that these non-state actors are immensely powerful in their relations. As we have said repeatedly, the field of strategy is too important to be left solely to the strategists.

References

Abbott, A. (1988) *The System of Professions: An Essay on the Division of Expert Labor*. Chicago: University of Chicago Press.

Ackroyd, S. (2007) The elephant in the room: some reflections of private equity. Talk presented at the 24 hours on strategy workshop. Aston Business School, 3–4 September.

Alvesson, M. (1993) Organisations as rhetoric: knowledge-intensive firms and the struggle with ambiguity, *Journal of Management Studies*, 30: 997–1015.

Alvesson, M. (2001) Knowledge work: ambiguity, image and identity, *Human Relations*, 54: 863–886.

Ansoff, I.H. (1965) *Corporate Strategy: An Analytic Approach to Business Policy for Growth and Expansion*. New York: McGraw-Hill.

Antonacopoulou, E. (2007) Practices, in S.R. Clegg and J.R. Bailey (eds), *The International Library of Organization Studies*. Thousand Oaks, CA: Sage, pp. 1291–1297.

Bachrach, P. and Baratz, M.S. (1962) Two faces of power, *The American Political Science Review*. December: 947–952.

Bachrach, P. and Baratz, M.S. (1970) *Power and Poverty: Theory and Practice*. New York: Oxford University Press.

Balogun, J. and Johnson, G. (2004) Organizational restructuring and middle manager sensemaking, *Academy of Management Journal*, 47(4): 523–549.

Barney, J. (1986) Types of competition and the theory of strategy: toward an integrative framework, *The Academy of Management Review*, 11(4): 791–800.

Barney, J.B. (1991) Firm resources and sustained competitive advantage, *Journal of Management*, 17(1): 99–120.

Barry, D. and Elmes, M. (1997) Strategy retold: toward a narrative view of strategic discourse, *Academy of Management Review*, 22: 429–452.

Bartlett, C. and Ghoshal, S. (1989) *Managing Across Borders: The Transnational Solution*. London: Century Press.

Beck, U. (1998) *World Risk Society*. Cambridge: Polity Press.

Beck, U. (2002) *Risk Society: Towards a New Modernity*. London: Sage.

Beck, U. (2006) *Cosmopolitan Vision*. Cambridge: Polity Press.

Behrendt, S. (2007) *The State of Business*. Available at: http://www.strategy-business.com/press/enewsarticle/enews103107, accessed March 25 2008.

Bevan, J. (2002) *The Rise and Fall of Marks and Spencer*. London: Profile Books.

Blackler, F., Crump, N. and McDonald, S. (2000) Organizing processes in complex activity networks, *Organization*, 7: 277–291.

Bourdieu, P. (1977) *Outline of a Theory of Practice*. Cambridge: Cambridge University Press.

Bourdieu, P. (1990) *The Logic of Practice*. Cambridge: Polity Press.

Braybrooke, D. and Lindblom, C.E. (1963) *A Strategy of Decision*. New York: Free Press.

Brown, J. and Duguid, P. (2000) *The Social Life of Information*. Boston, MA: Harvard Business School Press.

Brunsson, N. (1985) *The Irrational Organization: Irrationality as a Basis for Organizational Action and Change*. Chichester and New York: Wiley.

Burrell, G. (1996) *Pandemonium*. London: Sage.

Campbell, A. (2007) *The Blair Years*. London: Hutchinson.

Campbell, A. and Alexander, M. (1997) What's wrong with strategy?, *Harvard Business Review*, November–December: 42–50.

Carroll, L. (1982) *Alice's Adventures in Wonderland*. Oxford: Oxford University Press.

Carter, C. and Mueller, F. (2002) The 'Long March' of the management modernisers: ritual, rhetoric and rationality, *Human Relations*, 55(11): 1325–1354.

Carter, C. and Mueller, F. (2006) The colonisation of strategy: financialisation in a post-privatisation context, *Critical Perspectives on Accounting*, 17(8): 967–985.

Chaffee. E. (1985) Three models of strategy, *Academy of Management Review*, 10(1): 89–98.

Chandler, A. (1977) *The Visible Hand*. Cambridge, MA: Harvard University Press.

Chandler, A.D. (1962) *Strategy and Structure: Chapters in the History of the American Industrial Enterprise*. Cambridge, MA: MIT Press.

Child, J. (2002) Organizational structure, environment and performance: the role of strategic choice, in S.R. Clegg (ed.), *Central Currents in Organization Studies I: Frameworks and Applications* (Vol. 2). London: Sage, pp. 323–343. Originally published in *Sociology* (1972) 6: 1–21.

Clark, P. (2000) *Organisations in Action: Competition between Contexts*. London: Routledge.

Clark, T. and Fincham, R. (2002) *Critical Consulting: New Perspectives on the Management Advice Industry*. Oxford: Blackwell.

Clark, T. and Salaman, G. (1998) Telling tales: management guru's narratives and the construction of managerial identity, *Journal of Management Studies*, 35: 137–161.

Clausewitz, K. von (1968) *On War*. London: Penguin.

Clegg, S.B. (1989) *Frameworks of Power*. London: Sage.

Clegg, S.R. and Hardy, C. (1996) Representations, in S.R. Clegg, C. Hardy and W. Nord (eds), *Handbook of Organization Studies*. London: Sage, pp: 676–708.

Clegg, S.R. Courpasson, D. and Phillips, N. (2006) *Power and Organizations*. London: Sage.

Clegg, S.R., Kornberger, M. and Rhodes, C. (2005) Learning/becoming/organizing, *Organization*, 12(2): 147–167.

Clegg, S.R. and Kono, T. (2002) Trends in Japanese management: an overview of embedded continuities and disembedded discontinuities, *Asia Pacific Journal of Management*, 19(2–3): 269–285.

Cohen, M.D., March, J.G. and Olsen, J.P. (1972) The garbage can model of organizational choice, *Administrative Science Quarterly*, 17(1): 1–25.

Colville, I., Waterman, R. and Weick, K. (1999) Organizing and the search for excellence: making sense of the times in theory and practice, *Organization*, 6(1): 129–148.

Cooper, R. (1990) Organization/disorganization, in J. Hassard and D. Pym (eds), *The Theory and Philosophy of Organizations. Critical Issues and New Perspectives*. London/New York: Routledge, pp: 167–197.

Courpasson, D. (2002) Managerial strategies of domination: power in soft bureaucracies, in S.R. Clegg (ed.), *Central Currents in Organization Studies II: Contemporary Trends* (Vol. 5). London: Sage, pp. 324–345. Originally published in *Organization Studies* (2000) 21: 141–161.

Creveld, M. van (1999) *The Rise and Decline of the State*. Cambridge: Cambridge University Press.

Cruver, B. (2003) *Anatomy of Greed: The Unshredded Truth from an Enron Insider*. London: Carroll & Graf.

Cummings, S. (2003) *Recreating Strategy*. London: Sage.

Cunha, M., Clegg, S.R. and Kamoche, K. (2006) Surprises in management and organization: concept, sources and a typology, *British Journal of Management: Challenging Management Theory and Practice*, 17(4): 317–329.

Czarniawska, B. (2002) *A Tale of Three Cities: Or the Glocalization of City Management*. Oxford: Oxford University Press.

Czarniawska, B. (2005) Fashion in organizing, in B. Czarniawska and G. Sevón (eds), *Global Ideas: How Ideas, Objects and Practices Travel in the Global Economy*. Malmö/Copenhagen: Liber/CBS. pp. 129–146.

Czarniawska, B. and Sevón, G. (1996) *Global Ideas: How Ideas, Objects and Practices Travel in the Global Economy*. Oslo and Copenhagen: Liber and CBS Press.

De La Ville, V. and Mounoud, E. (2003) How can strategy be a practice? Between discourse and narration, in B. Czarniawska and P. Gagliardi (eds), *Narratives We Organize By*. Amsterdam: Benjamins. pp. 95–114.

De Certeau, M. (1984) *The Practice of Everyday Life*. Berkeley: University of California Press.

Derrida, J. (1990) *Some Statements etc*. Stanford: Stanford University Press.

Derrida, J. (1992) Force of law: the 'mystical foundation of authority', in D. Cornell, M. Rosenfeld and D. Carlson (eds), *Deconstruction and the Possibility of Justice*. New York/London: Routledge, pp. 3–67.

Derrida, J. (1995) *Points–Interviews 1974–1994*. Stanford: Stanford University Press.

Dertouzos, M., Lester, R.K. and Solow, R.M. (1989) *Made in America: Regaining the Productive Edge*. Cambridge and London: MIT Press.

Diamond, J. (2005) *Collapse: How Societies Chose to Succeed or Fail*. New York: Vintage.

Dierickx, I. and Cool, K. (1989) Asset stock accumulation and sustainability of competitive advantage, *Management Science*, 35: 1504–1511.

DiMaggio, P. and Powell, W.W. (2002) The Iron Cage revisited: institutional isomorphism and collective rationality in organizational fields, in S.R. Clegg (ed.), *Central Currents in Organization Studies I: Frameworks and Applications* (Vol. 3). London: Sage, pp. 324–362. Originally published in *American Journal of Sociology* (1983) 48: 147–160.

Dooley, R.S., Fryxell, G.E. and Judge, W.Q. (2000) Belaboring the not so obvious: consensus, commitment, and strategy implementation speed and success, *Journal of Management Studies*, 23(5): 501–517.

Durkheim, E. (1975) *Durkheim on Religion: A Selection of Readings with Bibliographies* (compiled by W.S.F. Pickering; new translations by Jacqueline Redding and W.S.F. Pickering). London: Routledge & Kegan Paul.

Easterby-Smith, M. and Lyles, M. (2003) *The Blackwell Handbook of Organizational Learning and Knowledge Management*. Oxford: Blackwell.

Eden, C. and Ackerman, F. (1998) *Making Strategy: The Journey of Strategic Management*. London: Sage.

Ezzamel, M. and Willmott, H. (2004) Rethinking strategy: contemporary perspectives and debates, *European Management Review*, 1(1): 43–48.

Fairbrother, M. (2007) Making neoliberalism possible: the state's organization of business support for NAFTA in Mexico, *Politics and Society*, 35(2): 265–300.

Flyvbjerg, B. (2001) *Making Social Science Matter: Why Social Inquiry Fails and How It Can Succeed Again*. Cambridge: Cambridge University Press.

Flyvbjerg, B. (2002) Bringing power to planning research: One researcher's praxis story, *Journal of Planning Education and Research*, 21(4) Summer: 353–366.

Foucault, M. (1977) *Discipline and Punish*. Harmondsworth: Penguin.

Friedman, M. (2002) *Capitalism and Freedom*. Chicago: University of Chicago Press.

Friedmann, J. (1998) The new political economy of planning: the rise of civil society, in M. Douglass and J. Friedmann (eds), *Cities for Citizens*. London: John Wiley.

Friedrich, C.J. (1937) *Constitutional Government and Politics*. New York: Harper and Bros.

Froud, J., Haslam, C., Johal, S. and Williams, K. (2000) Shareholder value and financialization: consultancy promises, management moves, *Economy and Society*, 29(1): 80–110.

Garfinkel, H. (1967) *Studies in Ethnomethodology*. Englewood Cliffs, NJ: Prentice-Hall.

Garrick, J. and Clegg, S.R. (2000) Organizational gothic: transfusing vitality and transforming the corporate body through work-based learning, in C. Symes and J. McIntyre (eds), *Working Knowledge: The New Vocationalism and Higher Education*. Buckingham: SRHE and Open University Press, pp. 153–171.

Geertz, C. (1973) *Interpretation of Cultures*. New York: Basic Books.

Gramsci, A. (1971) *Selections from the Prison Notebooks* (ed. and trans Quintin Hoare and Geoffrey Nowell-Smith). London: Lawrence & Wishart.

Grant, R. (1991) The resource-based theory of competitive advantage: implications for strategy formulation, *California Management Review*, 33(3): 114–135.

Giddens, A. (1984) *The Constitution of Society*. Cambridge: Cambridge University Press.

Hambrick, D.C. and Chen, M.-J. (2008) New academic fields as admittance-seeking social movements: the case of strategic management, *Academy of Management Review*, 33(1): 32–54.

Hambrick, D.C. and Fredrickson, J.W. (2001) Are you sure you have a strategy?, *Academy of Management Executive*, 15(4): 48–59.

Hamel, G. (1996) Strategy as revolution, *Harvard Business Review*, July–August: pp. 69–82.

Hamel, G. and Prahalad, C.K. (1990) The core competence of the corporation, *Harvard Business Review*, 68(3): 79–91.

Hardy, C., Palmer, I. and Phillips, N. (2000) Discourse as a strategic resource, *Human Relations*, 53: 1227–1248.

Harney, S. (2007) Strategy = management + Mao. Talk presented at the 24 hours on strategy workshop. Aston Business School, 3–4 September.

Hartcher, P. (2008) America's choice, our future, *Sydney Morning Herald*, February 8, http://www.smh.com.au/cgibin/common/popupPrint Article.pl?path=/articles/2008/02/07/1202234061869.html (accessed 25 March 2008).

Hatch, M. and Schultz, M. (2002) The dynamics of organizational identity, *Human Relations*, 55: 989–1019.

Haugaard, M. (2003) Reflections on seven forms of power, *European Journal of Social Theory*, 6(1): 87–113.

Hedberg, B., Nystrom, P. and Starbuck, W. (1976) Camping on seesaws: prescriptions for a self-designing organization, *Administrative Science Quarterly*, 21: 41–65.

Hendry, J. (2000) Strategic decision-making, discourse and strategy as social practice, *Journal of Management Studies* 37(7): 955–977.

Heracleous, L. (2003) *Strategy and Organisation: Realizing Strategic Management*. Cambridge: Cambridge University Press.

Heracleous, L. and Barrett, M. (2001) Organizational change as discourse: communicative actions and deep structures in the context of IT Implementation, *Academy of Management Journal*, 44(4): 755–778.

Hickson, D.J., Butler, R.J., Cray, D., Mallory, G.R. and Wilson, D.C. (1986) *Top Decisions: Strategic Decision-Making in Organizations*. San Francisco: Jossey-Bass.

Hickson, D.J., Miller, S.J. and Wilson, D.C. (2003) Planned or prioritized? Two options in managing the implementation of strategic decisions, *Journal of Management Studies*, 40(7): 1803–1836.

Hoskin, K. (2007) The ontology of strategy? Talk presented at the 24 hours on strategy workshop. Aston Business School, 3–4 September.

Hoskin, K. and MacVe, R. (1986) Accounting and the examination: a genealogy of disciplinary power, *Accounting, Organizations and Society*, 11(2): 105–136.

Hoskin, K. and MacVe, R. (1988) The genesis of accountability: the West Point connections, *Accounting, Organizations and Society*, 13(1): 3773.

Hoskin, K., MacVe, R. and Stone, J. (2006) Accounting and strategy: towards understanding the historical genesis of modern business and military strategy, in A. Bhimani (ed.), *Contemporary Issues in Management Accounting*. Oxford: Oxford University Press, pp. 165–190.

Hunter, J. and Cooksey, R. (2004) The decision to outsource: a case study of the complex interplay between strategic wisdom and behavioural reality, *Journal of Management and Organization*, 10(2): 26–40.

Jarzabowski, P. (2003) Strategic practices: an activity theory perspective on continuity and change, *Journal of Management Studies*, 40(1): 23–55.

Jarzabowski, P. (2004) Strategy as practice: recursiveness, adaptation and practices-in-use, *Organization Studies*, 25(4): 529–560.

Johnson, G., Melin, L. and Whittington, R. (2003) Micro-strategy and strategising, *Journal of Management Studies*, 40(1): 3–22.

Kallinikos, J. (1996) Mapping the intellectual terrain of management education, in R. French and C. Grey (eds), *Rethinking Management Education*. London: Sage, pp. 36–53.

Kallinikos, J. (2006) *The Consequences of Information: Institutional Implications of Technological Change*. Cheltenham: Edward Elgar.

Kallinikos, J. and Cooper, R. (1996) Writing, rationality and organization, *Scandinavian Journal of Management*, 12(1): 1–6.

Kierkegaard, S. (1992) *Concluding Unscientific Postscript 1: Kierkegaard's Writings*, Vol. 12.1. Princeton University Press.

Knights, D. (2002) Writing organization analysis into Foucault, *Organization*, 9(4): 575–593.

Knights, D. and Morgan, G. (1991) Corporate strategy, organizations, and subjectivity: a critique, *Organization Studies*, 12(2): 251–273.

Kono, T. and Clegg, S.R. (2001) *Trends in Japanese Management: Continuing Strengths, Current Problems, and Changing Priorities*. New York: Palgrave.

Learned, E., Christensen, C., Andrews, K. and Guth, W. (1969) *Business Policy: Text and Cases*. Homewood, IL: Irwin.

Liedtka, J. (2000) In defense of strategy as design, *California Management Review*, 42(3): 8–30.

Lindblom, C. (1959) The science of 'muddling through', *Public Administration Review*, 19(2): 79–88.

Lindblom, C.E. (1968) *The Policy-Making Process*. Englewood Cliffs, NJ: Prentice-Hall.

Luhmann, N. (1973) *Zweckbegriff und Systemrationalität. Über die Funktion von Zwecken in sozialen Systemen*. Frankfurt am Main: Suhrkamp.

Macaulay, S. (1966) *Law and the Balance of Power: The Automobile Manufacturers and Their Dealers*. New York: Russell Sage Foundation.

Machiavelli, N. (1988) *The Prince* (ed. Q. Skinner and R. Price). Cambridge: Cambridge University Press.

MacKenzie, D. (2006) *An Engine, Not a Camera: How Financial Models Shape Markets*. Cambridge, MA: MIT Press.

MacKenzie, D. (2007) The material production of virtuality: innovation, cultural geography and facticity in derivatives markets, *Economy and Society*, 36(3): 355–376.

McCloskey, D. (1985) *The Rhetoric of Economics*. Madison: University of Wisconsin Press.

McKinlay, A. (2002) The limits of knowledge management, *New Technology, Work and Employment*, 17(2): 76-88.

McLean, B. and Elkind, P. (2006) *The Smartest Guys in the Room: The Amazing Rise and Scandalous Fall of Enron Portfolio*. New York: Penguin Group.

March, J. (1971) The technology of foolishness, in J. March (ed.) (1988), *Decisions and Organizations*. Oxford: Blackwell. pp: 253–265.

March, J. (1981) Footnotes on organizational change, in J. March (ed.) (1988). *Decisions and Organizations*. Oxford: Blackwell. pp: 167–186.

Meyer, J.W. and Rowan, B. (1977) Institutionalized orgainzations: formal structure as myth and ceremony, *American Journal of Sociology* 83 (2): 340–363.

Miller, S.J. and Wilson, D.C. (2006) Perspectives on organizational decision-making, in S.R. Clegg, C. Hardy, T.B. Lawrence and W.R. Nord (eds), *The Sage Handbook of Organization Studies*. London: Sage, pp. 469–484.

Miller, S.J., Wilson, D.C. and Hickson, D.J. (2004) Beyond planning: strategies for successfully implementing strategic decisions, *Long Range Planning*, 37(3): 201–218.

Mintzberg, H. (1973) *The Nature of Managerial Work*. New York: Harper & Row.

Mintzberg, H. (1987) Five P's for Strategy, *California Management Review*, 30: 11–24.

Mintzberg, H. (1989) *Mintzberg on Management: Inside Our Strange World of Organizations*. New York: Free Press.

Mintzberg, H. (1990) The design school: reconsidering the basic premises of strategic management, *Strategic Management Journal*, 11: 171–195.

Mintzberg, H. (1994) *The Rise and Fall of Strategic Management*. New York: The Free Press.

Mintzberg, H. (1998) Five P's for strategy, in H. Mintzberg and B. Quinn (eds), *Readings in the Strategic Process*. Englewood Cliffs, NJ: Prentice-Hall, pp. 10–17.

Mintzberg, H. (2002) The organization as a political arena, in S.R. Clegg (ed.), *Central Currents in Organization Studies II: Contemporary Trends* (Vol. 5). London: Sage, pp. 50–69. Originally published in *International Studies of Management and Organizations* (1975) 1: 78–87; 20: 382–392.

Mintzberg, H. (2004) *Managers Not MBAs: A Hard Look at the Soft Practice of Managing and Management Development*. San Francisco: Berrett-Koehler.

Mintzberg, H., Ahlstrand, B. and Lampe, J. (1998) *Strategy Safari: A Guided Tour Through the Wilds of Strategic Management*. New York: Free Press.

Mintzberg, H., Raisinhani, D. and Theoret, A. (1976) The structure of 'unstructured' decision processes, *Administrative Science Quarterly*, 21: 246–275.

Moggach, D. (2000) *Tulip Fever*. London: Vintage.

Mosca, G. (1939) *The Ruling Class* (edited and revised, with an introduction by Arthur Livingston; translated by Hannah D. Kahn). New York: McGraw-Hill.

Mueller, F., Harvey, C. and Howorth, C. (2003) The contestation of archetypes: negotiating scripts in a UK Hospital Trust Board, *Journal of Management Studies*, 40(8): 1971–1995.

Munro, R. (2001a) Calling for accounts: numbers, monsters and membership, *The Sociological Review*, 49(4): 473-493.

Munro, R. (2001b) Unmanaging/Disorganization, *Ephemera: Critical Dialogues on Organization,* 1(4): 395-403.

Murray, W. and Grimsley, M. (1994) Introduction: on strategy, in W. Murray, K. MacGregor and A. Bernstein (eds), *The Making of Strategy: Rulers, States and War*. Cambridge: Cambridge University Press, pp. 1–8.

Nietzsche, F. (1968) *Basic Writings of Nietzsche*. New York: The Modern Library.

Nietzsche, F. (1974) *The Joyful Wisdom*. New York: Gordon Press.

Nonaka, I. and Takeuchi, H. (1995) *The Knowledge-Creating Company: How Japanese Companies Create the Dynamics of Innovation*. Oxford: Oxford University Press.

Nutt, P.C. (1984) Types of organizational decision processes, *Administrative Science Quarterly*, 29(3): 414–450.

Orwell, G. (1949) *Nineteen Eighty-Four*, a Novel. London: Secker & Warburg.

Pareto, V. (1968) *Applicazione di Teorie Sociologiche*. Totowa, NJ: Bedminster Press.

Pascale, R. (1999) Surfing the edge of chaos, *Sloan Management Review*, 40(3): 83–94.

Penrose, E. (1959) *The Theory of the Growth of the Firm*. Oxford: Basil Blackwell.

Peters, T. (2003) *Re-Imagine: Business Experience in a Disruptive Age*. London: Dorling Kindesley.

Peters, T. and Waterman, R. (1982) *In Search of Excellence: Lessons from America's Best-Run Companies*. Sydney: Harper & Row.

Pettigrew, A. (1973) *The Politics of Organizational Decision-Making*. London: Tavistock.

Pettigrew, A. (1985) *Awakening the Giant: Continuity and Change in ICI*. Oxford: Blackwell.

Pettigrew, A. (1997) What is a processual analysis?, *Scandinavian Journal of Management*, 13: 337–48.

Pettigrew, A. and Whipp, R. (1991) *Managing Change for Competitive Success*. Oxford: Blackwell.

Pitsis, T., Clegg, S.R., Marosszeky, M. and Rura-Polley, T. (2003) Constructing the Olympic dream: a future perfect strategy of project management, *Organization Science*, 14(5): 574–594.

Polanyi, M. (1967) *The Tacit Dimension*. New York: Anchor Books.

Polanyi, M. and Prosch, H. (1975) *Meaning*. Chicago: Chicago University Press.

Porter, M. (1980) *Competitive Strategy: Techniques for Analyzing Industries and Competitors*. New York: Free Press.

Porter, M. (1985) *Competitive Advantage: Creating and Sustaining Superior Performance*. New York: Free Press.

Porter, M. (1990) *The Competitive Advantage of Nations*. Basingstoke: Macmillan.

Porter, M. (1996) What is strategy?, *Harvard Business Review*, November–December: 61–78.

Porter, M., Stern, S. and Furman, J. (1999) The determinants of national innovative capacity, Harvard Business School Working Paper 00-034, 18 October.

Porter, M., Takeuchi, H. and Sakakibara, M. (2000) *Can Japan compete?* New York: Basic Books.

Power, M. (1997) *The Audit Society: Rituals of Verification*. Oxford: Oxford University Press.

Power, M. (2007) *Organized Uncertainty: Designing a World of Risk Management*. Oxford: Oxford University Press.

Priem, R. and Butler, J. (2001) Is the resource-based theory a useful perspective for strategic management research?, *Academy of Management Review*, 26(1): 22–40.

Pusey, M. (1991) *Economic Rationalism in Canberra: A Nation-building State Changes Its Mind*. Cambridge: Cambridge University Press.

Quinn, J.B. (1978) Strategic change: logical incrementalism, *Sloan Management Review*, 20(Fall): 7–21.

Quinn, J.B. (1980) *Strategies for Change: Logical Incrementalism*. Homewood, IL: Irwin.

Ray, T.E. and Clegg, S.R. (2007) Can we make sense of knowledge management's tangible rainbow? A radical constructivist alternative, *Prometheus*, 25(2): 161–185.

Ringland, G. (1998) *Scenario Planning: Managing for the Future.* Chichester: John Wiley & Sons.

Ringland, G. (2002) *Scenarios in Public Policy.* Chichester: John Wiley & Sons.

Ritzer, G. (2004) *The Globalization of Nothing.* Thousand Oaks, CA: Pine Forge Press.

Ross-Smith, A. and Kornberger, M. (2004) Gendered rationality? A genealogical exploration of the philosophical and sociological conceptions of rationality, masculinity and organization, gender, *Work and Organization*, 11(3): 280–305.

Salancik, G.R. and Pfeffer, J. (1974) The bases and use of power in organization decision-making: the case of the university, *Administrative Science Quarterly*, 19: 453–473.

Samra-Fredericks, D. (2003) Strategizing as lived experience and strategists' everyday efforts to shape strategic direction, *Journal of Management Studies*, 40(1): 141–174.

Schattschneider, E.E. (1960) *The Semi-Sovereign People: A Realists' View of Democracy in America.* New York: Holt, Rinehart & Winston.

Schatzki, T.R., Knorr-Cetina, K. and Von Savigny, E. (eds) (2001) *The Practice Turn in Contemporary Theory.* London and New York: Routledge.

Schumpeter, J. (1954) *The History of Economic Analysis.* Oxford: Oxford University Press.

Schutz, A. and Luckmann, T. (1973) *The Structures of the Life-World.* Evanston, IL: Northwestern University Press.

Schwenk, C.R. (1989) Linking cognitive, organizational and political factors in explaining strategic change, *Journal of Management Studies*, 26(2): 177–187.

Serres, M. (1982) *The Parasite.* Baltimore, MD: Johns Hopkins University Press.

Shaw, G. (2000) Planning and communicating using stories, in M. Schultz, M. Hatch and M. Larsen (eds), *The Expressive Organization. Linking Identity, Reputation, and the Corporate Brand.* Oxford and New York: Oxford University Press. pp. 182–195.

Shaw, G., Brown, R. and Bromily, P. (1998) Strategic stories: how 3m is rewriting business planning, *Harvard Business Review*, 76(3): 41–50.

Silverman, D. and Jones, J. (1976) *Organizational Work: The Language of Grading, the Grading of Language.* London: Collier Macmillan.

Simmel, G. (1950) 'The Stranger', *The Sociology of Georg Simmel.* New York: Free Press, pp. 402–408.

Simon, H.A. (1945) *Administrative Behavior,* 2nd edn. New York: Free Press.

Simon, H.A. (1960) *The New Science of Management Decisions.* New York: Harper & Row

Spender, J. and Scherer, A. (2007) The philosophical foundations of knowledge management: Editors' introduction, *Organization*, 14(1): 5–28.

Stalk, G. and Lachenauer, R. (2004) Hardball manifesto: five killer strategies for trouncing the competition, *Harvard Business Review*, April: 62–71.

Starbuck, W. (1983) Organizations as action generators, *American Sociological Review*, 48: 91–102.

Stein, H.F. (2001) *Nothing Personal, Just Business: A Guided Journey Into Organizational Darkness*. Westport, CT: Quorum Books.

Stern, S., Porter, M. and Furnham, M. (1999) The determinants of national innovative capacity, Harvard Business School Working Paper, 00–034.

Storey, J. and Barnett, E. (2000) Knowledge management initiatives: learning from failure, *Journal of Knowledge Management*, 4(2): 145–156.

Suarez-Villa, L. (1990) Invention, inventive learning, and innovative capacity, *Behavioral Science*, 35(4): 290–310.

Suchman, M.C. (1995) Managing legitimacy: strategic and institutional approaches, *Academy of Management Review*, 20(3): 571–610.

Sullivan, L.H. (1988) *Louis Sullivan: The Public Papers* (ed. Robert Twombly). Chicago and London: Chicago University Press.

Sun Tzu (2002) *The Art of War*. New York: Deodand Publishing.

Takeuchi, H. and Nonaka, I. (2004) *Hitotsubashi on Knowledge Management*. London: John Wiley.

Taleb, N. (2007) *The Black Swan: The Impact of the Highly Improbable*. New York: Random House.

Teece, D., Pisano, G. and Shuen, A. (1997) Dynamic capabilities and strategic management, *Strategic Management Journal*, 18(7): 509–33.

Thompson, A. and Strickland, A. (2006) *Strategic Management: Concepts and Cases*, 13th edn. London: McGraw-Hill.

Thornton, P. (2007) *Inside the Dark Box: Shedding Light on Private Equity*. London: The Work Foundation.

Thrift, N. (2006) Re-inventing invention: new tendencies in capitalist commodification, *Economy and Society*, 35(2): 279–306.

Tsivacou, I. (1996) The written form of planning, *Scandinavian Journal of Management*, 12(1): 69–88.

Tsoukas, H. (1998) Forms of knowledge and forms of life in organized contexts, in R. Chia (ed.), *In the Realm of Organization*. London: Routledge, pp. 43–66.

Tsoukas, H. (2003) Do we really understand tacit knowledge?, in M. Lyles and M. Easterby-Smith (eds), *The Blackwell Handbook of Organizational Learning and Knowledge Management*. Oxford: Blackwell, pp. 410–427.

Uchitelle, L. (2006) *The Disposable American: Layoffs and Their Consequences*. New York: Knopf.

Ullman, H.K. and Wade, J.P. (1996) *Shock and Awe: Achieving Rapid Dominance*. Available at: http://www.shockandawe.com/shockch2.html, accessed 18/12/07.

Van de Ven, A. (1992) Suggestions for studying strategy process, *Strategic Management Journal*, 13: 69–188.

Veyne, P. (1997) Foucault revolutionizes history, in A.I. Davidson (ed.), *Foucault and His Interlocutors*. Chicago, IL: University of Chicago Press. pp. 146–182.

Von Hayek, F. (1994) *The Road to Serfdom*. Chicago IL: University of Chicago Press.

Watzlawick, P. (1976) *How Real is Real?* New York: Random House.

Weick, K.E. (1979) *The Social Psychology of Organizing*, 2nd edn. Reading, MA: Addison-Wesley.

Weick, K.E. (1995) *Sensemaking in Organizations*. Thousand Oaks, CA: Sage.

Wernerfelt, B. (1984) A resource-based view of the firm, *Strategic Management Journal*, 5: 272–280.

Whipp, R. and Clark, P. (1986) *Innovations and the Auto-Industry: Product, Process and Work Organization*. London: Frances Pinter.

Whittington, R. (1992) Putting Giddens into action, *Journal of Management Studies*, 29(6): 693–712.

Whittington, R. (1996) Strategy as practice, *Long Range Planning* 29(5): 731–735.

Whittington, R. (2000) *What is Strategy – And Does it Matter?* (2nd edition). London: International Thomson Business Press.

Whittington, R. (2002) Practice Perspectives on Strategy: Unifying and Developing a Field, Best Paper Proceedings, Academy of Management, Denver.

Whittington, R. (2003) The work of strategizing and organizing: for a practice perspective, *Strategic Organization*, 1(1): 119–127.

Whittington, R. (2007) Strategy practice and strategy process: family differences and the sociological eye, *Organization Studies*, 28(10): 1575–1586.

Wittgenstein, L. (1972) *Tractatus Logico-Philosophicus*. London: Routledge & Kegan Paul.

Žižek, S. (2005) *Beyond Discourse Analysis, Interrogating The Real*. London: Continuum. pp. 271–284.

Index

Note: the letter 'f' after a page number refers to a figure and the letter 't' to a table.